The Anthony Hecht Lectures in the Humanities

Rome
and
Rhetoric

Shakespeare's *Julius Caesar*

Garry Wills

Yale UNIVERSITY PRESS   NEW HAVEN & LONDON

This book was first presented as the Anthony Hecht Lectures in the Humanities given by Garry Wills at Bard College in 2009. The lectures have been revised for publication.

Yale University Press books may be purchased in quantity for educational, business, or promotional use. For information, please e-mail sales.press@yale.edu (U.S. office) or sales@yaleup.co.uk (U.K. office).

Set in Janson type by Integrated Publishing Solutions, Grand Rapids, Michigan.
Printed in the United States of America.

Library of Congress Cataloging-in-Publication Data

Wills, Garry, 1934—
Rome and rhetoric : Shakespeare's Julius Caesar / Garry Wills.
      p.   cm.
Includes bibliographical references and index.
ISBN 978-0-300-15218-0 (cloth : alk. paper) 1. Shakespeare, William, 1564–1616. Julius Caesar. 2. Caesar, Julius—In literature. 3. Rhetoric, Renaissance.
4. Rome—In literature. I. Title.
PR2808.W58 2011
822.3′3—dc22
2011017965

A catalogue record for this book is available from the British Library.

This paper meets the requirements of ANSI/NISO Z39.48-1992 (Permanence of Paper).

10 9 8 7 6 5 4 3 2 1

The Anthony Hecht Lectures in the Humanities, given biennially at Bard College, were established to honor the memory of this preeminent American poet by reflecting his lifelong interest in literature, music, the visual arts, and cultural history. Through his poems, scholarship, and teaching, Anthony Hecht has become recognized as one of the moral voices of his generation, and his works have had a profound effect on contemporary American poetry. The books in this series will keep alive the spirit of his work and life.

To the memory of Anthony Hecht

Contents

Rome and Rhetoric

ONE

Caesar

Mighty Yet

To begin with Caesar is to begin with a puzzle. Why is it called *The Tragedy of Julius Caesar*? Why not *The Tragedy of Brutus*? Brutus, after all, speaks almost five times the number of lines that Caesar does. For that matter, Cassius has three times the words of Caesar. Antony has twice as many. Even the minor character Casca has almost as many lines (139) as Caesar does (155).[1] Caesar dies halfway through the play. Barbara Gaines, the director of the Chicago Shakespeare Theater, tells me it is hard to cast a great actor as Caesar. Who wants to perform half a play? (As we shall see, the great exception here was John Gielgud, with a definitive performance of the role in 1977.) When Caesar comes briefly back as a ghost, he speaks only sixteen words. What kind of play backs its main character off into a corner this way?

Cicero

I would like to wind my way into this problem with an even odder use of a character. Cicero is much on the minds of the play's conspirators. They talk almost obsessively about him, yet he is allowed to speak only nine measly lines. I will argue that the reasons for Caesar's small role and for Cicero's are connected. But first, consider how much people say about Cicero, who is held to almost total silence himself. In the first scene where Brutus speaks, he watches the company leave the site where Caesar was offered a crown. He describes the reaction of Cicero, which was obviously one of disgust at the charade:

The angry spot doth glow on Caesar's
   brow,
And all the rest look like a chidden train.
Calphurnia's cheek is pale, *and Cicero*
Looks with such ferret and such fiery eyes
As we have seen him in the Capitol
Being crossed in conference by some senators.
  (1.2.183–88)

Brutus wants to know more about Cicero's reaction to the offered crown. When Casca, who was
there, describes what happened, Brutus asks:

Did Cicero speak anything?
CASCA: Ay, he spoke Greek.
BRUTUS: To what effect?
CASCA: Nay, an I tell you that, I'll ne'er
look you i'th'face again. But those that
understood him smiled at one another, and
shook their heads; but for mine own part, it
was Greek to me. (1.2.278–84)

The whole point here was original in Shakespeare, since Plutarch expressly says that Casca did speak Greek. Shakespeare wanted to hint at some sardonic comment by Cicero without having to spell it out. It would make it harder for Brutus to exclude Cicero from the plot against Caesar if the orator's opposition to Caesar were too heavily emphasized. Plutarch repeatedly tells us that Cicero was famous for witty and cutting remarks, which made him many enemies.[2]

Since we are alerted to the fact that Cicero opposed the crowning of Caesar, we must wonder why he is not taken into the conspirers' circle. Whatever the ancient or modern views of Cicero, the Renaissance revered him as a champion of liberty and the republic. That is how he figures in Shakespeare's source, Plutarch. Every one of the conspirators against Caesar, all but Brutus, wants Cicero to be a confederate in their attempt.

> CASSIUS: But what of Cicero? Shall we sound him?
> I think he will stand very strong with us.

CASCA: Let us not leave him out.

CINNA: No, by no means.

METELLUS: O, let us have him, for his silver hairs

Will purchase us a good opinion

And buy men's voices to commend our deeds.

It shall be said his judgment ruled our hands.

Our youths and wildness shall no whit appear,

But all be buried in his gravity. (2.1.140–48)

Though Brutus excluded Cicero from the attack on Caesar, it was Cicero who made the most eloquent speeches (his so-called Philippics) against Antony when Antony became the champion of Caesar's legacy. And Plutarch treats Antony's revenge on Cicero as his most heinous crime:

And Antonius also commanded them to whom he had given commission to kill Cicero, that they should strike off his head and right hand, with the which he had written the invective Orations (called Philippides) against Antonius. So when the murtherers brought him Cicero's head and hand cut off, he beheld them a long time with great joy, and laughed heartily, and that oftentimes for the great joy he felt.[3]

That reflects a common view in antiquity, that Antony took a savage revenge on Cicero. The Roman poet Martial said that this guarantees that every tongue in the world will speak out against Antony.[4]

The shock of Cicero's death is registered in the play when Messala reports the proscriptions:

MESSALA: Octavius, Antony, and Lepidus
Have put to death an hundred senators.
BRUTUS: Therein our letters do not well agree.
Mine speak of seventy senators that died
In their proscriptions, Cicero being one.

CASSIUIS: Cicero one?
MESSALA: Cicero is dead,
And by that order of proscription.
(4.3.174–79)

Why, given Cicero's opposition to Caesar's faction as carried on by Antony, was he not included in the plot, where his judgment and white hairs could have justified the plotters' cause? Brutus gives his reason in the nighttime meeting at his orchard. When the others ask for Cicero to join them, he says:

O, name him not! Let us not break with him,
For he will never follow anything
That other men begin. (2.1.150–52)

That is not the reason given by Plutarch for excluding Cicero from the coup against Caesar. Plutarch says that Cicero is too fainthearted as well as too old—though Shakespeare's Metellus says that his old age would be an advantage to the younger conspirators. Brutus attributes to Cicero what is in fact his own failing—Plutarch said that *Brutus* could not be content to hold a second place.[5] Plutarch, while admitting that Cicero was vain about his own accomplishments, asserted that he was extraordinarily generous in recognizing the achievements of others, just the opposite of what Brutus alleges:

> Yet did he not malice or envy any other's glory, but would very frankly praise excellent men, as well those that had been before him, as those that were in his time. . . . There was not a famous man in all his time, either in eloquence, or in learning, whose fame he hath not commended in writing, or otherwise in honorable speech of him.[6]

The image of Cicero that Shakespeare wants for his play is the typical Renaissance attitude of respect for the champion of liberty. In the Renaissance, Cicero was at the peak of his reputation as the defender of the Republic, and that is how he was portrayed on the English stage of the time—

in Thomas Kyd's *Cornelia* (1594), the anonymous *Caesar's Revenge* (1595?), and Ben Jonson's *Catiline's Conspiracy* (1611).[7] In Shakespeare's play he makes an impressive figure in his one speaking appearance. In the midst of a storm, which has cowed the cheeky Casca, who first came on making smart-aleck comments, Cicero rebukes Casca's superstition:

> Indeed, it is a strange-disposed time.
> But men may construe things after their
>   fashion
> Clean from the purpose of the things
>   themselves. (1.3.33–35)

This fashioning of "construction" totally ("clean") divorced from reality shows that Cicero is an Academic, just as Plutarch said of him—a doubter of the certainties of most philosophical schools of his time. But the source of this pregnant passage, with the key use of the term "fashion," is a speech by the Epicurean Cassius in North's Plutarch. Shakespeare freely applies to one character in

his Roman plays what was said to or by another
character in Plutarch. When Brutus shows the
same kind of superstitious terror that Casca does
in the play, Cassius tells him:

In our [Epicurean] sect, Brutus, we have an
opinion that we do not always feel or see
that which we suppose we do both see and
feel; but that our senses, being credulous,
and therefore easily abused (when they are
idle and unoccupied in their own objects),
are induced to imagine they see and conjecture that which they in truth do not. For
our mind is quick and cunning to work
(without either cause or matter) anything in
the imagination whatsoever. And therefore
the imagination is resembled to clay and
the mind to the potter; who without any
other cause than his fancy and pleasure,
changeth it into what fashion and form
he will. And this doth the diversity of our
dreams shew unto us. For our imagination
doth, upon a small fancy, grow from conceit

to conceit, altering both in passions and forms of things imagined. For the mind of man is ever occupied; and that continual moving is nothing but an imagination. But yet there is a further cause of this in you. For you, being by nature given to melancholic discoursing, and of late continually occupied, your wits and senses, having been overlabored, do easylier yield to such imaginations. For, to say that there are spirits or angels, and if there were, that they had the shape of men, or such voices or any power at all to come unto us, it is a mockery.[8]

Since Shakespeare gives Cicero this dignified philosophical speech in his one brief speaking appearance, and since he has created a character others wonder about and connect with republican aspirations, why does Shakespeare bring him onstage only one earlier time, and then without letting him say a word?

This is the scene where Brutus and Cassius look

at the crowd coming back from the Lupercalia. Caesar and his train enlist almost all of the actors except the two who observe it pass. No one speaks as they go by until, at the end, Caesar tells Antony that Cassius is lean and dangerous. We know from Thomas Platter, the Swiss visitor to London in 1599, that the play's thirty-seven named characters were played by approximately fifteen actors, so some parts had to be doubled. Cicero does not speak at this appearance because the other character who doubles him when he appears later in the storm is onstage now. Thus Brutus describes the people passing by in what we should call a *teikhoskopia* ("ramparts view") technique. The word comes from the passage in Homer's *Iliad* where Helen, on the walls of Troy, identifies the Hellenic warriors deploying against the city. The scene is imitated by Virgil and Milton in their epics, but it is especially useful in plays, where offstage or silent action can be described.[9]

In *Julius Caesar*, the train of people goes by and then Caesar and Antony either hold up at the end to speak their lines, or actually come back to look

at Cassius, who had been absent from the Lupercalia. One of the people in the procession is clearly
the man who doubles as Cicero later on. Which
speaker is it, Caesar or Antony? Mere economy
would suggest that it is the one with fewer lines
(Caesar's 155 to Antony's 369). *Caesar and Cicero
are played by the same actor.* An indirect proof of
this doubling is that in modern productions where
doubling is not used, the use of a separate actor
to speak Cicero's few but impressive lines in the
storm is uneconomical—so the lines are dropped,
the actor eliminated.

Who then, in playing Caesar, doubled Cicero?
I suggest it was none other than Richard Burbage.
This goes against the general impression that Burbage would play the character with the most lines,
Brutus. But a consensus has now formed that in
the spectacularly busy 1599 season, *Julius Caesar*
was sandwiched between *Henry V* in the spring
and *Hamlet* in the fall.[10] Burbage would thus have
been rehearsing two of the longest roles in the
canon, Henry V and Hamlet, during their overlap
with *Julius Caesar*.[11] Shakespeare was letting him

get a comparative rest in this play, while using his major resource effectively. (Burbage undoubtedly played the lead role of Cicero in the 1611 *Catiline's Conspiracy* by Ben Jonson.)

Caesar

But is Caesar majestic in this drama? He is often played as a vain and foolish dictator, old if not decrepit, though Plutarch makes it a point to say that he was only fifty-six when he was murdered and that his health, despite his epilepsy, was vigorous, his physical skills outstanding (he could gallop a horse bareback with his hands behind him).[12] There is no reason to believe Cassius—in fact, there is good reason to reject him—when he describes Caesar's vulnerabilities to prod Brutus toward the assassination. His words about Caesar's pitifully weak begging for water and his flailing attempts at swimming say what Shakespeare knew from Plutarch was wildly false. Brutus' willingness to believe such lies shows that he was predisposed to despise Caesar already. This is what Shakespeare knew of Caesar, and of the great loyalty his troops felt for him:

They did not wonder so much at his valiantness in putting himself at every instant in such manifest danger, and in taking so extreme pains as he did—knowing that it was his greedy desire of honor that set him afire and pricked him forward to do it—but that he always continued all labor and hardnesses, more than his body could bear, that filled them all with admiration. For, concerning the constitution of his body, he was lean, white and soft-skinned, and often subject to headache, and otherwhile to the falling sickness (the which took him the first time, as it is reported, in Corduba, a city of Spain) but yet therefore yielded not to the disease of his body, to make it a cloak to cherish him withal, but contrarily took the pains of war as a medicine to cure his sick body, fighting always with his disease, travelling continually, living soberly, and commonly lying abroad in the field.[13]

Cassius' defiance of reality is proved when he says that Caesar was so poor a swimmer that he had to save him. Plutarch tells us that when Caesar's men were in danger off the shore of Alexandria, Caesar leaped into a boat to rescue them, and when his boat went down, he not only saved himself by swimming with one hand, but held books above the water with his other hand.

He leaping into the sea, with great hazard saved him self by swimming. It is said that, then holding divers books in his hand, he did never let them go, but kept them always upon his head above water and swam with the other hand, notwithstanding that they shot marvelously at him, and he was driven sometime to duck into the water.[14]

Suetonius repeats the story of that famous event.[15] Caesar's swimming skills were widely celebrated in antiquity, as by Appian in *Civil Wars* 2.150:

> In his war at Alexandria, when stranded
> on a bridge with danger all around, he
> threw off his purple cloak and dove into
> the sea. With his foes on the lookout for
> him, he burrowed underwater for a great
> distance, surfacing rarely to snatch a breath
> of air, until he reached a friendly ship and,
> waving his arms, showed himself and was
> saved.

Though swimming was no part of the athletic/ military training in Greece, it was respected as a martial art in Rome. Plutarch praises Cato the Elder for the way he taught his son "to storm his way through the swirls and surges of Tiber."[16] When Nero plotted to kill his mother by sinking the ship she was on, that tough woman outwitted him by swimming to safety.[17] The differing heroic ideals can be seen in the fact that the shipwrecked Odysseus rides a bit of his ship's timber while his Greek troops drown, but Aeneas's Romans swim in the waters that whelmed their boat.[18]

Plutarch, admittedly, criticizes Caesar as ambitious, but he praises his courage, leadership, and skill. Taking over frightened troops in Gaul, he earns their trust by joining the front line of infantry, sending off the horse that could carry him out of danger, saying he would ride from the battlefield only after taking a horse from the defeated enemy. When, later, his men hesitate to take on larger numbers of German fighters, he says he will go forward alone, with only his loyal Tenth Legion, which shames the rest into continuing their fight.[19]

Plutarch says that Caesar was resented less for his own ambition than for the arrogant behavior of his soldiers, and especially of Mark Antony, in acquiring riches for themselves.[20] Shakespeare shows that he had noticed this claim in Plutarch when he makes Brutus say:

What, shall one of us
That struck the foremost man of all this
world
But for supporting robbers . . . (4.2.73–75)

Plutarch, moreover, believed it was a good thing that Caesar founded an empire—Plutarch not only lived under the Roman Empire (in its conquered Greek territory), but considered that empire divinely ordained:

Caesar's power and government, when it came to be established, did indeed much hurt, at his first entry and beginning, unto those that did resist him: but afterwards unto them that, being overcome had received his government, it seemed he rather had the name and opinion only of a tyranny than, otherwise, that he was so in deed. For there followed not any tyrannical nor cruel act but, contrarily, it seemed that he was a merciful physician whom God had ordained,

of special grace, to be Governor of the
Empire of Rome, and to set all things again
at quiet stay, the which required the coun-
sel and authority of an absolute Prince. And
therefore the Roman people were marvel-
ous sorry for Caesar after he was slain.[21]

Brutus himself says he cannot ascribe any tyrannical act to Caesar.

> Th'abuse of greatness is when it disjoins
> Remorse from power. And to speak truth of
>   Caesar,
> I have not known when his affections
>   swayed
> More than his reason. (2.1.18–21)

Caesar is played as vainglorious in most modern
productions. But some of his boasts are a matter
of Roman honor. When, for instance, Artemidorus
tells Caesar to look first at his document, since
it concerns Caesar's own safety, Caesar grandly
replies

20

What touches us ourself shall be last
served. (3.1.8)

This has been called the tragic flaw that leads to
Caesar's death—he refuses to learn of the conspiracy against him, thinking he is invulnerable.
When he dismisses another plea, he preens himself on being able to turn down requests:

These couchings and these lowly courtesies
Might fire the blood of ordinary men . . .
If thou dost bend and pray and fawn for
   him
I spurn thee like a cur out of my way.
   (3.1.35–36, 45–46)

This attitude does not seem attractive to most
modern audiences. But Plutarch praises Brutus for
having the same willingness to reject petitions:

For as Brutus' gravity and constant mind
would not grant all men their requests
that sued unto him but, being moved with

reason and discretion, did always incline to that which was good and honest. . . . For, flattering of him, a man could never obtain anything at his hands, nor make him to do that which was unjust. Further, he thought it not meet for a man of calling and estimation to yield unto the requests and entreaties of a shameless and importunate suitor requesting things unmeet: the which notwithstanding, some men do for shame, because they dare deny nothing. And therefore he was wont to say that he thought them evil brought up in their youth that could deny nothing.[22]

The modern world does not much like monarchs —unless, like the modern monarchs of England, they are powerless. But that was not the attitude of Plutarch under the Roman emperor or of Elizabethans under their queen. Shakespeare had just finished a play glorifying the monarch Henry V when he wrote *Julius Caesar*, and the historiography of his time honored Caesar.[23] Ben Jonson in *Sejanus* has to make clear that the play's hero does not oppose Tiberius for being an emperor but for being a cruel and evil emperor:

> Men are deceiv'd who think there can be
>   thrall
> Beneath a virtuous prince. Wish'd liberty
> Ne'er lovelier looks than under such a
>   crown.[24]

According to Plutarch, the gods appointed Caesar as Rome's physician, and their displeasure is proved by the avenging spirit that appeared to Brutus.[25] Francis Bacon, in his essay on revenge, argues that private revenge is wrong, but not public revenge for treason. "Public revenges are for the most part fortunate, as that for the death of Caesar."[26] According to Plutarch, Caesar was killed because of the excesses of his soldiers and friends—especially Mark Antony.[27] But Bacon said Caesar fell because he was too forgiving of his foes—he had spared both Brutus and Cassius after they warred on him—which was the judgment rendered in antiquity by (for instance) Appian.[28]

Caesar is given special greatness by contrast with the man he is paired with in the "parallel lives" technique of Plutarch. Alexander and Caesar are linked as great conquerors, both brave, ambitious, and imbued with a sense of destiny. The life of Caesar is not complete as it comes down to us—it lacks the opening paragraphs and the formal comparison of the two men at the end of the dyad. But it is clear that Caesar would have come off the better of the two from what Plutarch writes of Alexander—that he put himself above the law (52), made others kiss the ground before him (74), succumbed to superstition and heavy drinking (75). Caesar was too trusting of his friends, Alexander too suspicious (74). We cannot know for sure that Shakespeare read the entire dyad, but he read around in Plutarch seeking plot material. There is no reason to think he read only the lives he finally took plays from—he would not have known what would give him material until after he had read it. At any rate the picture in Plutarch is completed by the contrast between Caesar and Alexander. (It is interesting that Caesar is a strong swimmer in Plutarch, and Alexander cannot swim at all [58].)

Caesar was a commanding figure in the Renaissance imagination. He should be played that way in Shakespeare's drama. Otherwise the power of his specter to haunt all the later action of the play makes no sense. Burbage had to make Caesar a figure to reckon with. To present him, as so often happens now, as a tinpot dictator or a dithering old fool is to reduce the scale of the tragedy. This accepts Cassius' lies to Brutus as, in effect, internal stage directions on how to play the man, whereas what Antony says about Caesar in the funeral oration is, according to Plutarch, true—his triumphs, his bequests to the state and the citizenry, his grain for the poor.[29] It is not only Antony who calls him "the noblest man / That ever lived in the tide of times" (3.1.256–57). Brutus says that he and Cassius "struck the foremost man of all this world" (4.3.22). Brutus says that Cassius would not have dared to scold Caesar as he has done him (4.3.59). Both men tell Caesar's mighty spirit it is avenged (5.3.45, 94, 5.5.50).

In Plutarch, Caesar is so powerful—just the opposite of the timorous weakling Cassius describes —that the whole gang of assassins cannot bring him down:

> Then Casca behind him strake him in the
> neck with his sword, howbeit the wound
> was not great nor mortal because, it seemed,
> the fear of such a devilish attempt did
> amaze him, and take his strength from him,
> that he killed him not at the first blow. But
> Caesar, turning straight unto him, caught
> hold of his sword and held it hard: and they
> both cried out, Caesar in Latin: "O vile
> traitor, Casca, what doest thou," and Casca
> in Greek to his brother, "Brother, help me."
> At the beginning of this stir, they that were
> present, not knowing of the conspiracy,
> were so amazed with the horrible sight they
> saw that they had no power to fly, neither

to help him, nor so much as once to make
any outcry. They on the other side, that
had conspired his death, compassed him in
on every side with their swords drawn in
their hands, that Caesar turned him nowhere but he was stricken at by some, and
still had naked swords in his face, and was
hacked and mangled among them as a wild
beast taken of hunters. For it was agreed
among them, that every man should give
him a wound, because all their parts should
be in the murther: and then Brutus himself
gave him one wound about his privities.
Men report also, that Caesar did still
defend himself against the rest, running
every way with his body: but when he saw
Brutus with his sword drawn in his hand,
then he pulled his gown over his head, and
made no more resistance, and was driven
either casually, or purposedly by the coun-
sel of the conspirators, against the base
whereupon Pompey's image stood, which
ran all of a gore blood till he was slain.

Thus, it seemed that the image took just revenge of Pompey's enemy being thrown down on the ground at his feet and yielding up his ghost there, for the number of wounds he had upon him. For it is reported, that he had three and twenty wounds upon his body: and divers of the conspirators did hurt themselves, striking one body with so many blows.[30]

Shakespeare could not have this wild chase all over the stage. He had to have the killers huddle tight about the (rare) stage property, the statue of Pompey, since the basin of "blood" was secreted there, for them to bathe their hands and swords in it, and to pull out a bloodied cloak to throw over the body (for later use by Antony at the funeral). But the blood vivid on all their hands gave the scene its violent shock effect. Shakespeare tries to suggest the wild scene when he says that Caesar was given thirty-three stabs (5.1.53), rather than the twenty-three Plutarch reports, though Shakespeare has only six men stabbing. And while the killers do not wound each other in the mayhem as Shakespeare describes it, he does give a sense of the struggle when Antony says that their daggers "Hacked one another in the sides of Caesar" (5.1.40).

The murder scene is a fulfillment of Calphurnia's dream:

> She dreamt tonight she saw my statue,
> Which like a fountain with an hundred
>   spouts
> Did run pure blood. And many lusty Romans
> Came smiling, and did bathe their hands in
>   it. (2.2.76–79)

That vision is eerie enough; but Decius Brutus gives it an even more surreal twist, trying to reassure Caesar:

> This dream is all amiss interpreted.
> It was a vision fair and fortunate.
> Your statue spouting blood in many pipes,
> In which so many smiling Romans bathed,

Signifies that from you great Rome shall
    suck
Reviving blood, and that great men shall
    press
For tinctures, stains, relics, and cognizance.
    (2.2.83–89)

This dream, along with its interpretation, is not in Plutarch or any other Shakespeare source. It is wrenched in tabloid fashion from current events. The execution of traitors in the 1590s was gory in the extreme—the hanged man had his entrails and heart cut out, his body cut down while he was still alive, his head cut away and his four limbs "quartered." Since the most famous of these executions involved Jesuit priests, Catholics pressed around the scaffold where blood was everywhere and dipped cloths into the blood to carry away as "first-class relics" of their saints. The relics of Henry Garnet were gathered at his scaffold, after his execution for involvement in the Gunpowder Plot. They would become famous and were hunted for by the king's agents. But the relics of earlier

priests—Edmund Campion and Robert Southwell
—were also treasured by Catholics and resented
or reviled by the authorities. Samuel Johnson
understood the reference: "The Romans, says
Decius [Brutus], all come to you as to a saint, for
reliques."[31]

The religious resonance around Caesar's death
is an ironic echo of Brutus' attempt to make the
assassination a religious sacrifice.[32] Antony, in the
funeral oration, predicts that Decius' false story
about "tinctures, stains, relics, and cognizance" will
prove true, once Romans read the will of Caesar.
Then indeed they will

> dip their napkins in his sacred blood,
> Yea, beg a hair of him for memory
> And, dying, mention it within their wills,
> Bequeathing it as a rich legacy
> Unto their issue. (3.2.133–37)

Brutus had said that the blood spouting from
Caesar was a fountain of freedom. In fact, the men
who seal themselves with Caesar's blood are marked

for retaliation. It is a curse, not a blessing—in any case, a sacrament of some kind of doom. Plutarch says:

> His great prosperity and good fortune, that favored him all his life time, did continue afterwards in the revenge of his death, pursuing the murtherers both by sea and land, till they had not left a man more to be executed of all them that were actors or counselors in the conspiracy of his death.[33]

Cassius wanted to convince Brutus that the apparently invincible Caesar, bestriding the world like a Colossus, was in fact weak and vulnerable, a fainthearted target. But in fact the killers made him more powerful, gave him posthumous strength, made him stride across seas and lands like a Colossus of retribution. The stricken power is stronger than ever. Shakespeare makes Caesar's spirit stalk his killers in the most vivid way. The ghost that appears to Brutus in Plutarch is his own evil

genius—*ho sos daimon kakos* (*Brutus* 36), "ton mau-
vais ange" in Amyot, "your ill angel" in North.
It is not Caesar who comes to avenge himself in
this source. Rather, it is "a wonderful strange and
monstrous shape of a body coming toward him."[34]
Shakespeare, by contrast, makes Caesar himself
the stalking vengeance. Shakespeare may have
taken this idea of Caesar's ghost from *Caesar's Revenge*, if (as seems likely) that play preceded his.
And the hunted men that spirit stalks recognize
who is bringing them down. Cassius is killed with
the instrument he used on Caesar. He says:

> Caesar, thou art revenged
> Even with the sword that killed thee
> (5.3.45–46)

And Brutus dies with these words on his lips:

> Caesar, be still.
> I killed not thee with half so good a will
> (5.5.50–51)

The spirit of Caesar takes over his victims. Cassius had attacked Caesar for aspiring to a crown, but he dies wearing one himself, after Titinius has crowned his corpse; "Look wheth'r he have not crowned dead Cassius" (5.3.97). Cassius had mocked Caesar's supposed physical infirmities, but he fails to see what has happened on the battlefield because "My sight was ever thick" (5.3.21). Calphurnia was frightened by omens and portents, an attitude Cassius scorned as an Epicurean. But by the end of the play he says, "Now I change my mind / And partly credit things that do presage" (5.1.77–78). Caesar was censured because his troops seized treasure. But Brutus' honor is besmirched by Cassius' pilferings (4.3.23–26), and Brutus' own troops disrupt the battle by seeking private loot (5.3.7). As these killers enact what they rebuked in Caesar, the spirit of Caesar looks on, triumphant.

When John Gielgud played the role of Caesar in 1977, reviewers said that he seemed to speak as the ghost with a voice of doom. "Bernard Levin wrote . . . that 'his "Ay," at Philippi hovered in the air like some infinitely shimmering echo.'"[35] In fact, Gielgud's performance that year, directed by John Schlesinger, seems to have hit just the note that Shakespeare wanted and Burbage could deliver: David Daniell writes: "Gielgud's Caesar had such great natural authority that his spirit was obviously unconquerable from the start."[36] Marvin Spevack agrees: "Gielgud . . . endowed the titular hero with a great natural authority, and it was clear from the outset that the conspirators would not be able to conquer his spirit. Caesar's ghost haunted the battle scenes."[37] Brutus at last gets it right when he says:

> O Julius Caesar, thou art mighty yet,
> Thy spirit walks abroad and turns our swords
> In our own proper entrails. (5.3.94–96)

The role of Caesar is short, measured by the number of his spoken lines. He is, nonetheless, the presiding spirit of the play. Everything turns around him. The role that was good enough for Burbage proved good enough for the great Gielgud.

Brutus

Rhetoric Verbal and Visual

Brutus' Funeral Oration

Shakespeare's Brutus is not often treated as a rhetorician because, at Caesar's funeral, he is out-orated by Mark Antony. But rhetoric had many uses and abuses in the Elizabethan image of Rome, and Shakespeare's Brutus is at the very center of that enigma. The historical Brutus was very interested in rhetoric. Cicero dedicated two of his treatises on the subject to Brutus.[1] We know we are in Rome as we watch *Julius Caesar* because everyone is talking Roman—Roman oratory and rhetoric about Roman virtue and power. Of course, all of Shakespeare is highly rhetorical. As Brian Vickers notes, "The period roughly between [Philip] Sidney and George Herbert sees the flowering of rhetoric in English literature. More new textbooks of rhetoric were produced in that period than any other."[2] Wolfgang Müller writes that rhetoric is so massively present throughout English Renaissance poetry that it is hard to distinguish *ars poetica* from *ars rhetorica*.[3] In *Love's Labor's Lost*, rhetoric as a subject is even more emphasized than in *Julius Caesar*. But there the rhetoric is made up of verbal tricks and playfulness. Oratory in *Julius Caesar* has serious political import—it can make or unmake the state. The *suasoria*, an exercise in persuasive declamation, drives the action.[4] Cassius persuades Brutus that Caesar must die, Brutus persuades himself that Caesar must die. Calphurnia persuades Caesar not to go to the Senate before Casca persuades him to go. Portia produces her thigh wound as a persuasive gesture, and Antony produces the bloody cloak of Caesar as a persuasive gesture. As John W. Velz observes,

"Portia in nightdress uses the rhetoric of the Forum to address her husband about their domestic life."[5] The tribunes sway the mob in the play's opening scene before Antony does so in the funeral scene. Brutus and Cassius engage in mutual execration in the tent scene. If these are verbal games, the games have the highest stakes.

The characters here speak the way Elizabethan schoolboys were taught that Romans had spoken. The Latin training in Shakespeare's time was highly rhetorical. Colin Burrow calls the protreptic address of the goddess in *Venus and Adonis*

a glorified version of the *suasoriae* (or formal speeches of persuasion) which Shakespeare is likely to have practised at Stratford Grammar School. . . . [He] probably had an extensive training in the art of rhetoric at school, where he is very likely to have been required to imagine speeches which would fit particular characters, and to argue on either side of a complex question, such as whether or not it is a good thing to marry.

A commonplace of the art was that rhetoric
was a form of irresistible power (a frequent
emblem for rhetoric in this period was that
of an orator dragging his audience around
by golden chains tied to their ears).[6]

At the Canterbury school attended by Christopher Marlowe, the curriculum stated: "In the Fifth
Form they shall commit to memory the [rhetori-
cal] figures."[7] These "figures"—variously called
ornaments, schemata, tropes—were signature devices of the ancient orators: anaphora, polyptoton,
khiasmos, ploke, homoioteleuton, isokola, and on
and on.[8] There were scores of them, all mounted
like butterflies in book after book.[9] Cicero said,
"Figures both of speech and of thought are almost uncountable."[10]

Jean Fuzier finds thirty "figures" crowded into
Brutus' short funeral oration.[11] Because the speech
is so brief, and because it is in prose, and because
Shakespeare read in Plutarch that Brutus prac-
ticed the Laconic style in his letters, and because
Antony's following speech is so highly emotional,

it is easy to think that Brutus' speech is plain and simple by comparison. It is not. It is as contrived and artificial as Shakespeare could make it.

Its opening weave of words has what Fuzier (28) calls a combination of *epanalepsis* (beginning and ending a clause with the same word), and *epiphora* (ending successive clauses with the same word):

> *Hear* me for my cause,
> > and be silent that you may *hear*.
> *Believe* me for mine honor,
> > and have respect to mine honor that you
> > may *believe*.
> *Censure* me in your wisdom,
> > and awake your senses that you may the
> > better *judge*. (3.2.12–17)

Angel Day (96) and Richard Sherry (59) would analyze this opening as a case of "*metastasis* or *transitio*," which Day defines as "when in brief words we pass from one thing to another."[12] It is a kind of ladder climb, from rung to rung, as Day's example shows—an example very like Brutus' opening steps.

> You have heard by this what you ought to
>   consider; hear now, I pray you, what you
>   are bound to remember.
> These things you will say are pleasant, but
>   the rest untold are far more delightful.
> This already showed unto you seems to be
>   tolerable, that which follows is no way to
>   be suffered.
> I have now told you what was done in
>   private, I will next show you what was
>   handled in public . . .

Chiasm

The artful contrivance of Brutus' opening sentences is not exhausted with those analyses. Lurking in them is the ghost of one of the most intricate figures, the chiasm—what the Greeks (and most Elizabethans) also called *antimetabole* ("reverse

interchange").[13] The Greek *khiasmos* was named
for the letter *khi* (chi, X), since the four elements
of the figure mimic the shape of the letter if they
are arranged to bring out their crisscross relationship (a-b, b-a). The illustration most often used by
Renaissance writers on rhetoric came from Quintilian's treatise *Rhetorical Training*:

> I LIVE not in order to *eat*
>   but *eat* in order to LIVE.[14]

This was a device against which the rhetoricians
warned, since it was so obviously contrived. Hoskyns, who devoted a whole book to the study of
Sir Philip Sidney's *Arcadia*, notes (128–29) that

> Our learned knight [Sidney] slipped often
> into this figure . . . yet he conceived [ar-
> ranged] the particularity [oddity] of his
> affection [affectation] by this: sometimes
> by not turning the words wholly back as
> they lay [e.g.]

> To account it not a purse for treasure,
> but as a treasure itself worthy to be
> pursed up . . .
>
> Sometime the same sense must be in
> contrary words, as—
>
>> Parthenia desired above all things to have
>> Argalus, Argalus feared nothing but to
>> miss Parthenia—
>
> where "fear to miss" is put instead of
> "desire to have."

Hoskyns warns that this figure, like alliteration ("rhymes running in rattling rows"), can easily be overdone:

> Notwithstanding that this is a sharp and
> witty figure, and shows out of the same
> words a pithy distinction of meaning
> very convenient for schoolmen, yet Mr.
> P[layfere] did wrong to tire this poor
> figure by using it thirty times in one
> sermon.[15] For use of this or any other
> point unseasonably, it is as ridiculous

as it was in the fustion oration, "horse-
mill, mill-horse," etc.[16] But let discretion
be the greatest and general figure of
figures.

Theodore Sorensen liked this figure when he was
writing speeches for President Kennedy: "Let us
never negotiate out of fear, but let us never fear to
negotiate." Or: "Ask not what your country can
do for you; ask what you can do for your country."
Or: "Only when our arms are sufficient beyond
doubt can we be certain beyond doubt that they
will never be employed."

Shakespeare mocked the silly use of chiasm, as
in Polonius' "'Tis true, 'tis pity. / And pity 'tis, 'tis
true. A foolish figure" (2.2.97–98), and "The cause
of this defect, / For this effect defective comes by
cause" (2.2.101–2). It can be a sign of euphuistic
artificiality, as in the play within the play, *The Murder of Gonzago:*

Where little fears grow great,
Great love grows there. (3.2.167)

45

Grief joys, joy grieves. (3.2.194)

Whether love lead fortune or else fortune
    love. (3.2.198)

The device can show a clown's muddled brain—
Launce says, "They have pitched a toil; I am toil-
ing in a pitch"—*Love's Labor's Lost* 4.3.2. In the
same play, when Boyet uses a chiasm, the Princess
calls it a "painted flourish" (2.1.14). In *Twelfth
Night*, when Viola uses it, Feste says such rever-
sals are like a "cheveril glove"—"how quickly the
wrong side may be turned outward" (3.1.10–11).
Tracy Lord in Philip Barry's *The Philadelphia Story*
calls this a "corkscrewing of words." And its artificiality makes modern song lyricists love to play
with it. So Irving Berlin writes:

I'm fancy free
    and free for anything fancy.

Or Yip Harburg dangles this before us:

When I'm not facing the face that I fancy,
  I fancy the face I face.

When the device is used for deadly purpose, it
can suggest a confusion of order, as in *Richard III*
(1.3.71–72):

Since every Jack became a gentleman,
There's many a gentle person made a jack.[17]

Macbeth's witches, who personify confusion, say
"Fair is foul and foul is fair" because they live with
"th'equivocation of the fiend" (5.5.43). We saw
that Hoskyns considered the chiasm "very con-
venient for the schoolmen [scholastics]," which
was not a compliment at the time, since Renaissance rhetoricians were largely influenced by Peter
Ramus, who rejected the scholastic logic. Berowne
in *Love's Labor's Lost* (4.3.284) is asked by his as-
sociates to supply them with "some tricks, some
quillets how to cheat the devil" (by evading their
own oaths). He comes up with a whole firecracker-

string of sophistical chiasms to defend equivocation
—which he later admits is a way to "play foul play
with our oaths" (5.2.750), a bit of Jesuitry for
which the Princess imposes a heavy penance on
him.[18] There is often something suspect about the
chiasm, at least when it is used in a concentrated
way—as it is in the opening of Brutus' speech:

> HEAR me for my *cause*,
>> and be *silent* that you may HEAR.
> BELIEVE me for mine *honor*,
>> and have respect to mine *honor* that you
>> may BELIEVE.
> CENSURE me in your *wisdom*,
>> and awake your *senses* that you may the
>> better JUDGE.[19]

The speech that opens with this density of "figures" proceeds in the same vein throughout.

Partitio

Later in the speech, Shakespeare uses another figure he often mocked, the *partitio* or *divisio*, which

breaks down a theme into its parts, often with an indication of the speaker's intended way of dealing with each item. Seneca the Elder made "division" one of the three main subjects of his rhetorical *summa* (the other two being maxims and colors).[20] Hoskyns (136) said this figure is "like the shows which peddlers make of their packs."[21] Francis Bacon called it a form of the rhetorical figure *amplificatio* (expansion): "A way to amplify anything is to break it, and to make anatomy of it in several parts, and to examine it according to several circumstances."[22]

A joke on the device and the term is in *Midsummer Night's Dream*, where Demetrius says that Snout, playing the wall, which is itself a partition, makes the "wittiest partition" in showing his parts:

In this same interlude it doth befall
That I, one Snout by name, present a wall;
And such a wall as I would have you think
That had in it a crannied hole, or chink,
Through which the lovers, Pyramus and
   Thisbe,

Did whisper often, very secretly.
This loam, this rough-cast, and this stone
    doth show
That I am that same wall—the truth is so—
And this the cranny is, right and sinister,
Through which the fearful lovers are to
    whisper. (5.1.154–63)

Shakespeare can make his clowns parade ridicu-lous "partitions."[23] Itemizing is often a mark of the pedantic, the pseudo-pedantic, or of one sati-rizing pedagogy—Olivia ticking off her points of beauty, Falstaff the specific things honor cannot do, Jaques the different ages of man, Dromio the geographical parts of a woman's body, Phoebe the charms of the disguised Rosalind, Moth the various parts of love, or Dogberry the crimes of his captive.[24] Such laying out of the cards is often silly. It is not much less foolish when Polonius does the partitioning:

To expostulate
What majesty should be, what duty is,

Why day is day, night night, and time is
  time,
Were nothing but to waste night, day, and
  time. (2.2.86–89)

The comic partition turns unexpectedly cruel in
Julius Caesar when the mob catechizes poor Cinna
the poet:

1 PLEBEIAN: What is your name?

2 PLEBEIAN: Whither are you going?

3 PLEBEIAN: Where do you dwell?

4 PLEBEIAN: Are you a married man or
a bachelor?

1 PLEBEIAN: Answer every man
directly.

2 PLEBEIAN: Ay, and briefly.

3 PLEBEIAN: Ay, and wisely.

4 PLEBEIAN: Ay, and truly, you were
best.

POET: What is my name? Whither am I
going? Where do I dwell? Am I a married
man or a bachelor? Then to answer every

man directly and briefly, wisely and truly.
Wisely, I say I am a bachelor. (3.3.5–16)

He does not begin with his name, Cinna, for that
would be the end of the catechesis.

The surprising thing is to see Brutus spreading
his cards the same way. Here is a classic *partitio*:

As Caesar *loved* me, I weep for him,
as he was *fortunate*, I rejoice at it.
as he was *valiant*, I honor him.
but as he was *ambitious*, I slew him.
There is tears for his *love*;
joy for his *fortune*;
honor for his *valor*;
and death for his *ambition*.
Who is here so *base* that would be a
    bondman?
        If any, speak; for him have I
    offended.
Who is here so *rude* that would not be
    Roman?

> If any, speak; for him have I
> offended.
> Who is here so *vile* that will not love his
> country?
> If any, speak; for him have I offended.
> (3.2.24–34)

It is all very cut and dried, pedantically so. Don J. Kraemer says this *partitio* "verbally carves Caesar up."[25]

Another figure is being used here, too—*taxis.*[26] Antithesis pairs things as obvious opposites. Taxis links things as obvious adjuncts. So Brutus pairs tears with love, joy with fortune, honor with valor, and death with ambition. Finally, of course, he lines up a series of rhetorical questions. The rhetorical question does not call for an answer. But Brutus' questions actually forbid an answer. He says that anyone he offends should speak up—but only if they are base, rude, or vile. This is questioning as bullying. Kraemer rightly characterizes "the thought-numbing uniformity of Brutus'

polished figures."[27] Brutus layers his figures, in-
terlaces them, piles them up, runs one through
another, violating the teaching of Quintilian: "Figures, no matter how good in themselves, should
not be crowded together. This makes them obvious, so they end up being both obnoxious and
unconvincing."[28]

Brutus' speech has usually been treated re-
spectfully in the critical literature on this play.
But its rhetoric is so overdone that it approaches
what is comic elsewhere in Shakespeare. And
there is another thing to notice about it. It is all
about himself. Antony's speech will be all about
Caesar—what he conquered, how he loved, what
he leaves his countrymen. But in the speech of
Brutus there is a monotonous dwelling on Brutus,
his honor, his unquestionable standing. He asserts that Caesar was ambitious, but gives no
shred of evidence for this. His saying so is sufficient. To doubt the assertion would be to question the unquestionable—Brutus' integrity. Go
over the speech again with that in mind.

Hear **ME** for **MY** cause, and be silent that
you may hear. Believe **ME** for **MINE**
honor, and have respect to **MINE** honor
that you may believe. Censure **ME** in your
wisdom, and awake your senses that you
may the better judge. If there be any in this
assembly, any dear friend of Caesar's, to
him **I** say that **BRUTUS'** love to Caesar
was no less than his. If then that friend
demand why **BRUTUS** rose against
Caesar, this is **MY** answer. Not that **I** loved
Caesar less, but that **I** loved Rome more.
Had you rather Caesar were living, and die
all slaves than that Caesar were dead, to live
all free men? As Caesar loved **ME, I** weep
for him. As he was fortunate, **I** rejoice at it.
As he was valiant, **I** honor him. But as he
was ambitious, **I** slew him. . . . Who is here
so base that would be a bondman? If any,
speak; for him have **I** offended. Who is
here so rude that would not be a Roman?
If any, speak; for him have **I** offended. Who

is here so vile that will not love his country?
If any, speak; for him have **I** offended. . . .
With this **I** depart, that as **I** slew **MY** best
lover for the good of Rome, **I** have the
same dagger for **MYSELF** when it shall
please **MY** country to need **MY** death.

Brutus' sublime self-absorption is expressed as he
leaves but tells the crowd to stay behind as he leaves:
"For **MY** sake, stay here with Antony" (3.2.57).

His emphasis on his own honor will give Antony the cue to dwell sardonically on the "honorable men" who killed Caesar, just as it gave Cassius the key to lead Brutus about by the nose
(1.2.92, 309):

Well, honor is the subject of my story.

Thy honorable mettle may be wrought.

Brutus' honor, his supposed strength, is actually his
weakness. It is the instrument of self-involvement,
as we can see from the chiasmic form itself. It is

not a forward-moving argument, like a syllogism, but a circling back upon itself: "Believe me for *my honor*, and have respect to *mine honor* that you may believe." He does not go out to others to convince them, but asks the audience to come into his own conviction of his own perfection—that is not something they are to be persuaded of, but something they are to *believe*. Those who do not believe are not just wrong. They are so *base*, so *rude*, so *vile* as to challenge his virtue and perfection.

Prose Artifice

Some claim that the speech of Brutus is brief and sincere, and either "Stoic" or "Laconic," because it is contrasted with the "demagogic" speech that follows it. Brutus' short and packed oration has even been compared with the Gettysburg Address. But prose is not a guarantee of authenticity in Shakespeare. Quite the opposite. We tend in our literary culture to think of prose as authentically unstudied and "everyday," while verse is artificial and "worked up." But when Shakespeare's people speak with genuine emotion, of love or hate or something else, they do so in poetic form. Shakespeare's world is like that imagined by Chesterton, where poetry is the natural expression, prose the unnatural:

> The great error consists in supposing that poetry is an unnatural form of language. We should all like to speak poetry at the moment when we truly live, and if we do not speak it, it is because we have an impediment in our speech. It is not song that is the narrow or artificial thing, it is conversation that is a broken and stammering attempt at song. . . . The poetic does not misrepresent the speech one half so much as the speech misrepresents the soul.[29]

In Shakespeare, prose is reserved for things *less* authentic—obtuseness in clowns, disorderliness in fools, subversiveness in Falstaff, officiousness in documents, or indirectness in letters. None of these is a "purer" voice of the speaker. When Henry V reads a document, or Horatio reads a letter, that is reported in prose. I would suggest that to all the other contrasts between the speeches of Brutus and Antony—brevity vs. expansiveness, prose vs. verse, self-involvement vs. outreach, quick but shallow acceptance vs. emotional upheaval—we should add this: Brutus *reads* his cold and studied text. Brian Vickers came close to concluding this when he wrote,

> [Brutus begins with an] almost detachable opening such as many rhetoricians (Cicero and Bacon, to go no further) advised the orator to have ready prepared. . . . Immediately before his oration and immediately after it Brutus speaks verse, so suggesting that this is a prepared speech, penned and learned in a vacuum, oblivious to the audience response to it either during or after its delivery.[30]

Vickers shrewdly sees the whole problem of Brutus' oration as foreseen by Quintilian in his *Rhetorical Instruction:*

> The first consideration is what the situation
> calls for, what the audience, what the time,
> since the whole point of these figures is
> their acceptability. When, after all, the
> contention is a matter of atrocity, hostility,
> or compassion, who wants to hear outrage,
> lament, or pity presented in antitheses, neat
> cadences, and comparisons? Verbal nicety
> here undermines the basis of trust, and
> makes truth disappear in the ostentation
> of artifice.[31]

The use of prose for this speech is all the more striking in that the rest of the play has an extraordinarily high incidence of verse. Indeed, only four other plays (all early, and two with *no* prose) have fewer prose lines than this one.[32] That makes it more certain that Shakespeare wanted to make this prose speech anomalous, one more proof of

Brutus' fatal miscalculations. Brutus is certain that he will control the people. Antony will use many different arguments and emotional appeals when he speaks. Brutus is certain he needs only one— his own honor, which it is inconceivable to him that anyone can question. All his rhetorical tricks are pasted on as ornament to this one basic point.

The Orchard Soliloquies

The artifice of Brutus shows in his most "inward" speeches, the soliloquies in his orchard. They are often presented as a struggle with himself over the killing of Caesar. They are not. At the very beginning of the first one he says to himself, "It must be by his death." He is not about to reason why. It is decided. Raskolnikov does not reason to the killing of the pawn broker. On the first page of *Crime and Punishment*, he admits that the idea is just lodged in him, he knows not how. It should be noted that Brutus' declaration of murderous intent is made *before* Lucius brings him the papers forged by Cassius that urge him to the deed. Brutus never argues, with Cassius or with himself, over killing Caesar. In Macbeth's soliloquy at a similar point before a murder, he raises objections to killing Duncan—the king's status as a guest, his merit and virtues. To his wife Macbeth says, at one point, "We'll proceed no further." Brutus never says that to Portia, to Cassius, to himself, to anyone.

The soliloquy in the orchard is not over whether to act, but how to present the action to others. The terms of the discussion are those of rhetoric— terms like "common proof" and "quarrel" and "color" and "fashion." The key passage is this:

> And since the quarrel
> Will bear no color for the thing he is,
> Fashion it thus . . . (2.1.28–30)

A "quarrel" is, in rhetoric, a dispute to be presented from either side, the ground of a *controversia*.[33] A "color" is a plausible presentation on either side. It is in this sense that Holofernes says, "I do fear colorable colors" (*Love's Labors Lost* 4.2.149).

Francis Bacon wrote a little treatise, *Of the Colours of Good and Evil* (1597), in which he presented ten fallacies with which a case can be "colored." The word "color" is one Shakespeare was encountering often while he worked on this play. It was a favorite term of Thomas North, who made the translation of Plutarch on which Shakespeare was relying. North usually means by it an "excuse" or "disguise"—he uses it in those senses seven times in *The Life of Julius Caesar* alone, the last two times as rationalizations for killing Caesar.[34]

Some uses of colors, Bacon admitted, can be legitimate, if they simply reinforce reasonable grounds for conviction. But the more common use of a color is to cover a weak argument, whereby a "persuader" uses "colors, popularities and circumstance which are of such force as they sway the ordinary judgment whether of a weak man, or of a wise man not fully and considerately attending and pondering the matter."[35] "Popularities" are, in this context, crowd-pleasing saws—Bacon was putting the odd word "popularity" into common use at just this time, often using it to mean

something like demagogy.[36] Michael Winterbottom, in his edition of Seneca's book on maxims,
divisions, and colors, describes color as "a method
of interpreting the facts that was to the advantage
of the speaker."[37] In modern political parlance we
call this "spin." Quintilian uses it for what would
later be called "casuistries."[38]

We have already seen one of the *topoi* Bacon
refers to in his little treatise, that of *partitio*. Bacon
says it is fallacious to argue that itemizing a matter necessarily makes it more compelling. The
colors, too, he says, are "places of persuasion
and dissuasion," where "places" are *topoi*, *loci*, or
common*places*—what Brutus in the orchard calls
a "common proof" (2.1.21). In *The Rape of Lucrece*
(267) Tarquin scorns any justification of his rape:
"Why hunt I then for *color* or excuses?" Cleopatra
tells Antony to stop giving excuses for leaving
her: "Seek no color for your going" (*Antony and
Cleopatra* 1.3.32).

Since Brutus says "the quarrel will bear no color
for the thing he [Caesar] *is*," one must allege what
he *might become*—one of the fallacious "colors"

condemned by Bacon, "the commonplace of extolling [exaggerating] the beginning of anything." This is what might be called the fallacy of inception, or "the slippery slope." Seneca writes: "This color is reprehended [refuted] in such things which have a natural course and inclination contrary to an inception. So that the inception is continually evacuated and gets no start."[39] The fallacy, he says, confuses a process from potentiality to actuality with a process from actuality to augmentation, or mistakes a process from impotence to potentiality as a process from potentiality to act. In other words, it treats a hypothetical (tyranny) as an inevitability, and (in Brutus' case) commits an *actual* assassination in the name of that *hypothetical* tyranny.

So Brutus must "fashion it thus"—force or feign the matter. We have seen Cicero in this play describe fanciful interpretations: "Men may construe things after their fashion" (1.3.34). Brutus will say that he can manipulate Ligarius as he wishes: "Send him but hither and I'll fashion him" (2.1.220). Thus Brutus "fashions" the assassination by using the kinds of "places" that Bacon called suspect.

> It is the bright day that brings forth the
>   adder. (2.1.14)
>   But 'tis a common proof
>   [*locus communis*]
> That lowliness is young ambition's ladder.
>   (2.1.21–22)

> And therefore think him as a serpent's egg
> Which, hatched, would as his kind grow
>   mischievous. (2.1.32–33)

This piling up of maxims (*sententiae*) is something Quintilian condemned:

> They make for a broken-up speech, since
> each maxim stands apart, and one must
> start over when each one ends. . . . Such
> neat and rounded maxims do not intercon-
> nect. . . . No matter how flashy each is on
> its own, they do not make a single confla-

gration, but separate sparks in a smoky haze, and they have no impact in a truly luminous speech, as the stars disappear in daylight.[40]

The second soliloquy is even more revealing. While contemplating the killing of a (would-be) king, he presents his own inner turmoil as the dethroning of his own kingly control:

Since Cassius first did whet me against
    Caesar
I have not slept.
Between the acting of a dreadful thing
And the first motion, all the interim is
Like a phantasma or a hideous dream.
The genius and the mortal instruments
Are then in council, and the state of man,
Like to a little kingdom, suffers then
The nature of an insurrection. (2.1.61–69)

Cassius' first "whetting," his first sharpening of the assassin's knife in Brutus' mind, is the first "motion"—like the motion in a parliament—to a dreadful act, prompting the hideous dream of what must be done. The guiding spirit of this motion (the genius) then goes into planning at a "council" with its death-dealing means (its "mortal instruments"). These are in a plot against the inner "little kingdom," an insurrection, an inner revolt against the ruling principle of the psyche. The *political* language for the speaker's psyche is worked out in great detail. Brutus makes himself an inner object of the plot that he is outwardly planning against Caesar. This reveals the false consciousness of his immediately preceding soliloquy. The killing of Caesar is a projection of his own kingly conception of himself. The idea that he is Caesar's son killing his father is already suggested here, to be developed more fully in the tragic consequences of this regicide-parricide.

Visual Rhetoric

The fact that Brutus thinks in terms of rhetorical presentation is seen in many ways. He recommends dissimulation; he feigns reluctance to the deed he is urging; he arranges a pageant of the blood to dramatize that he and his fellow conspirators are liberators. He constructs a visual as well as a verbal rhetoric. He says of the conspiracy:

> Hide it in smiles and affability,
> For if thou path, thy native semblance on,
> Not Erebus itself were dim enough
> To hide thee from prevention. (2.1.82–85)

This was something Shakespeare found in North's Plutarch: "When he was out of his house, he did so frame and *fashion* his countenance and looks that no man could discern he had anything to trouble his mind."[41] This is the advice Lady Macbeth gives her husband:

>   To beguile the time
> Look like the time—bear welcome in your
>   eye,
> Your hand, your tongue; look like
>   th'innocent flower,
> But be the serpent under't. (1.5.62–65)

The conspirators, Brutus says, must pretend they did not want to do what they did.

> And let our hearts, as subtle masters do,
> Stir up their servants to an act of rage
> And after seem to chide 'em.
>   (2.1.174–76)

David Daniell, in his Arden edition, points out that nineteenth-century performers, trying to idealize Brutus, regularly cut this recommendation of a feigning conduct, as if the noble Brutus were a Machiavel pretending, like Richard III, to chide his own agents.

Brutus puts on a false face not only before possible foes but before friends, as we can see from his pretence to be hearing of his wife's death for the first time at 4.3.179 ff. Though he has already told Cassius of her death, he pretends to have heard nothing of it when Messala reports it. When told that "For certain she is dead," he strikes a heroically stoic pose:

Why, farewell Portia. We must die,
  Messala.
With meditating that she must die once
I have the patience to endure it now.
  (4.3.188–90)[42]

Brutus wants to hide his inner self not only from others but from himself. He wants to ethe-realize the assault on Caesar, making it only a murder of the mind:

We all stand up against the spirit of Caesar,
And in the spirit of men there is no blood.
Oh that we then could come by Caesar's
  spirit
And not dismember Caesar. (2.1.166–69)

He tries to cover up the ugly reality with ritual pieties:

Let us be sacrificers, but not butchers,
  Caius. . . .

Let's kill him boldly but not wrathfully.
Let's carve him as a dish fit for the gods,
Not hew him as a carcass fit for hounds. . . .
We shall be called purgers, not murderers.
  (2.1.166, 172–75, 180).

Purgers, not murderers? Sacrificers, not butchers?
Carvers who do not hew? Brutus is performing a
kind of transubstantiation, turning blood back into
sacrificial wine.

  It was to deny the ugly realities of the plot that
Brutus refused to treat it as a contract, swearing
an oath to kill Caesar:

No, not an oath. If not the face of men,
The sufferance of our souls, the time's abuse,
If these be motives weak, break off betimes,
And every man hence to his idle bed.
  (2.1.113–16)

The conspirators are not murderers acting on
their own motives. They are just following popu-

lar demand ("the face of men," as Johnson saw, means their countenancing the act), their own mistreatment ("the sufferance of our souls"), and historical pressure ("the time's abuse").[43] They are the instruments of a historical inevitability. Like Marxian agents, they are wielded by historical forces, the necessary flow of events.

After the murder—pardon me, "the sacrifice"— Brutus continues to make the tangible blood a mere symbol of the spirit. Now that he and the others are spattered with the real thing, their hands and daggers steeped in it, since they are unable to deny its reality—to wash it out, as Lady Macbeth tries to do—Brutus says that they should in effect *bathe* in it, as a sacramental stuff, not carnal, not "encarnadining." Shakespeare gives us a parodic version of the Book of Revelation (7:14): They "have washed their robes, and made them white in the blood of the lamb." The Roman conspirators hide, with their choreography of death, the basin of fake blood behind Pompey's statue in which they dip their hands.

> Stoop, Romans, stoop,
> And let us bathe our hands in Caesar's
> blood
> Up to the elbows, and besmear our swords.
> Then walk we forth even to the market
> place,
> And waving our red weapons o'er our
> heads,
> Let's all cry, "Peace!" "Freedom!" And
> "Liberty!" (3.1.105–10)

When Antony comes before the assassins, he turns their bloody symbols against them. He draws attention to their killers' hands, not cloaking them in sacrificial terminology.

> I do beseech ye, if you bear me hard,
> Now, whilst your purple hands do reek and
> smoke,
> Fulfill your pleasure. (3.1.157–59)

Brutus tries to return to the *spiritual* meaning of the murder, dismissing bloody externals:

> Though now we must appear bloody and
>   cruel,
> As by our hands and this our present act
> You see we do, yet see you but our hands,
> And this the bleeding business they have
>   done.
> Our hearts you see not. They are pitiful.
> (3.1.165–67)

Antony will pun on their "hearts" as the hart (deer) they hunted, though Brutus said they would not kill Caesar as a carcass brought down by hounds.

Taking the cue of Brutus' own reference to their hands, Antony now takes every hand solemnly, one by one, sealing his own right hand in the blood he will avenge. It is done in a counterritual to the one they indulged in as they bathed each hand in Caesar's blood. In formal procession from man to man, Antony says:

> Let each man render me his bloody hand.
> First, Marcus Brutus, will I shake with you.
> Next, Caius Cassius, do I take your hand.

[I imagine Cassius reluctantly giving up his
    hand, since he suspects what Antony is
    doing.]
Now, Decius Brutus, yours. Now yours,
    Metellus,
Yours, Cinna. And, my valiant Casca, yours.
[Does he hesitate before that "valiant,"
    since Casca struck from behind?]
Though last, not last in love, yours, good
    Trebonius. (3.1.184–89)

Did Shakespeare remember a similar ritual-revenge
scene, from early in his career, when Titus Andronicus vows to avenge his two murdered sons
and his ravaged daughter? The text says simply:

You heavy people, circle me about,
That I may turn me to each one of you
And swear unto my soul to right your
    wrongs. (3.1.277–79)

Some editors suppose that Titus shakes his one
remaining hand with each son, and touches his

76

ravished daughter's head. But Jonathan Bate imagines a bloodier ritual, using Titus' severed hand and his sons' decapitated heads.[44]

When Antony goes in solemn motion from man to man, he holds captive each hand that struck at Caesar, checking it in a retributive stillness. This antiritual, countering Brutus' blessing of the hands' work, is followed by a kind of liturgical gloss on the action:

> Shall it not grieve thee, dearer than thy
>   death,
> To see thy Antony making his peace,
> Shaking the bloody fingers of thy
>   foes—
> Most noble—in the presence of thy
>   corse? (3.1.196–99)

Brutus is convinced that his staging of the matter will explain it entirely. When Cassius cautioned him against letting Antony speak over Caesar's body, Brutus dismissed the mere idea that any person would question his virtue.

I will myself into the pulpit first,
And show the reason of our Caesar's death.
  (3.1.236–37)

Brutus has only one thing in mind throughout. As Plutarch puts it, "Brutus did not trust so much to the power of his army as he did to his own virtue."[45] It was a slender thing to lean on.

Antony

The Fox Knows Many Things

Brutus' speech at Caesar's funeral hammered home one argument—that his own honor had to be relied on. Mark Antony deploys a vast variety of persuasive devices. Lawyers have for centuries debated these differing approaches. Most of them think that, in appealing to a jury, every conceivable argument should be deployed, since the pleader never knows which one will affect this or that juror. Abraham Lincoln, on the other hand, when arguing a case at law, puzzled some onlookers by conceding point after point, certain that if the nub of a case were established, the jurors must agree on it.[1]

These two tactics are now, thanks to a 1953 essay by Isaiah Berlin, discussed often in terms of a line from the Greek poet Arkhilokhos: "Many things the fox knows, the hedgehog one, but big."[2] Francis Bacon, unlike Berlin, relied on a different Greek author— Aesop rather than Arkhilokhos:

> So likewise hereupon Aesop framed the fable of the fox and the cat—whereas the fox bragged what a number of shifts and devices he had to get from the hounds, and the cat said he had but one, which was to climb a tree, which in proof [experience] was better worth than all the rest. Whereof the proverb grew, *Multa novit vulpis, sed felis unum magnum* [The fox knows many things, the cat one, but big]. . . . So it falleth out to be a common error in negotiating—whereas men have many reasons to induce or per-suade, they strive commonly to utter and use them all at once, which weakeneth

them. For it argueth, as was said, a needi-
ness in every of the reasons by itself, as if
one did not trust to any of them, but fled
from one to another, helping himself only
with that: *Et quae non prosunt singula, multa
juvant* [Things that do not work one by one
prevail combined]. Indeed, in a set speech
in an assembly, it is expected a man should
use all his reasons in the case he handleth,
but in private persuasions it is always a
great error.[3]

Antony goes against Bacon's advice (and Lincoln's practice). He wins in his contest with Brutus, but this may be because the one thing Brutus
knew, his own honor, was not "big" in this arena—
he did not get to the real nub. In any event, Antony's multiple approach is stunningly effective.
He does not, as Bacon thought, show the insuffi-
ciency of any one approach by his refusal to rely
upon it. Rather, his different rhetorical devices
play into and strengthen one another. He passes
the only test that matters in classical rhetoric—

audience response. As Cicero put it, "The effect of the orator is in the affect of his hearers" (*efficiatur ut afficiantur*).[4] Cicero also said that logic is like a fist, while persuasion is like an outstretched hand.[5] Brutus with his tight argument waved a fist. Antony will open both his hands to the crowd.

The rhetorical devices relied on by Antony are quite different from those used by Brutus. The chiasm, which came fairly naturally to the antithetical Greek style, looked more forced in Latin and very artificial in English. That is why Shakespeare so often treated it as "a foolish figure" (in Polonius' words). Besides, Brutus piles figure on figure in a crammed little space. Antony moves at a more relaxed pace through a *development* of different figures—*ironia, praeteritio, interrogatio, anaphora,* and *aposiopesis*. It is paradoxical that chiasm, which has a rounded QED quality as a kind of logical trap, should be considered unpersuasive, while irony, which says the opposite of what it means, should be considered a pathway to truth.

The explanation for this apparent anomaly is given by Cicero, who wrote: "Irony, a deft and elegant figure, is what people attribute to Socrates."[6] The Socrates of Plato made denial of knowledge a preparation for knowledge. It is a device, misleading on the surface, that reveals the disparity between appearance and reality. When Socrates says, "I know you are wise, so tell me this," he is undermining the claims to wisdom in his interlocutor. When Antony says that he knows Brutus is honorable, he is using the textbook example of irony as was taught in the Renaissance. We have these models of irony in the rhetorical handbooks:

1512:   Erasmus, *De Copia:* "My good man."

1550:   Richard Sherry, *A Treatise of Schemes and Tropes:* "You are an honest man."

1577:   Henry Peacham, *The Garden of Eloquence:* "You did like an honest man."

1586:   Angel Day, *The English Secretarie:* "You are an honest man."

1589:   George Puttenham, *The Arte of
English Poesie:* "No doubt you are a
good man."

When Antony says, "So are they all, all honorable men," it would raise the immediate sugges-
tion that he was speaking as these rhetoricians did.
On the face of it, he is just joining Brutus in the
affirmation of his own honor:

> Believe me for mine honor,
> And have respect to mine honor that you
> may believe.

But Antony means to pry open the tight circular-
ity and self-ratification in that sentence. He will
cite and appeal to that honor, continuing to af-
firm it against the odds, as the honor begins to look
more and more threadbare each time he invokes
it. Antony should not begin with a sneering tone.
The vulnerability of the claims should emerge
gradually from the dissonance with each new context in which Antony places them. Eight times we

are assured of Brutus' honor, and each time the title teeters more ominously.

The second device relied on by Antony is *interrogatio*, the rhetorical question. Brutus had used this figure, but not to admit an answer.

Who is here so *base* that would be a
    bondsman?
—so *rude* that would not be a Roman?
—so *vile* that would not love his country?

Speak, that is, if you are contemptible. (If not, then shut up.) His questions do not go deeper into the subject at hand, but close the matter before response is possible.

Antony's questions are meant to elicit a response, whether voiced or internal:

He hath brought many captives home to
    Rome
Whose ransoms did the general coffers fill—
Did this in Caesar seem ambitious?
    (3.2.89–91)

Well, no, not that, the audience may grant. But what about—Antony anticipates such a response, and is out ahead of it:

> I thrice presented him a kingly crown,
> Which he did thrice refuse—was this
>   ambition? (97–98)

Well, no. Not that, either.

Antony's strategy alternates concession and challenge. Yes, Brutus is honorable—we must begin with that, as the one sure thing. But he says his honor drove him to rebuke ambition—and just what was Caesar's ambitious action? Was it here? Was it there? This burrowing under a conceded point, while repeating the concession, is Socratic. Socrates says, "I realize that you know all about virtue. So surely you can tell me this little thing about it. No? Well, what about this other little thing?" The Socratic aim is to reduce confidence, inducing disorientation, leading to *aporia*, a puzzled halt. This engages the interlocutor in a *process* of enquiry, a dialogue moving from one mental state to another. Shakespeare found this dialectic interplay suggested in Plutarch's description of Antony's speech.

> When he saw that the people were very glad and desirous also to hear Caesar spoken of, and his appraises uttered: he mingled his oration with lamentable words, and by amplifying of matters did greatly move their hearts and affections unto pity and compassion.[7]

Plutarch's life of Brutus makes even clearer the interplay between Antony and the crowd.

> Antonius making his funeral oration in praise of the dead, according to the ancient custom of Rome, and *perceiving that his words moved the common people to compassion, he framed his eloquence to make their hearts yearn the more.*[8]

Antony reads his audience—he waits for the basis to take his next step. He moves with them, building on their reactions. He has engaged them in a joint enquiry.

All right, he says, Caesar must have been ambitious, since the honorable Brutus says so. Even that statement is more deeply ironic by this time:

> The noble Brutus / Hath told you . . .
>   (77–78)
> But Brutus says . . . (86)
> Yet Brutus says . . . (93)
> Yet Brutus says . . . (99)

From being an endorsement, Brutus' testimony becomes a kind of involuntary self-accusation, its emptiness signaled by the sheer repetition of the barren formula: *Ipse dixit*. A quiet counterview is gaining strength under all these professions of "honor."

> I speak not to disprove what Brutus spoke
>   . . . (100)
> I will not do them wrong . . . (125)
> I fear I wrong the honorable men . . . (151)

And then: "Shall I descend?" (160). Brutus gave orders to the crowd. "Believe me! Speak if you dare! Stay here! Listen to Antony!" By contrast, Antony asks the crowd's permission to go on, to read the will, to descend. Like Socrates, Antony claims not to impose knowledge but to elicit it from his hearers' own capacities. "I tell you that which you yourselves do know" (214).

To the dialectical devices of irony and interrogation Antony adds, as the speech moves toward its climax, *praeteritio*, the device that emphasizes a point by saying the orator will not mention it. As the ghost says in Jonson's *Catiline*, "Thy incest with thy sister I not name" (1.42). The rhetoricians treated this as a form of irony—it says the opposite of what it means, and it has the heuristic value of challenging appearances, opening a gap between words and reality. Antony's *praeteritio* plays changes on the idea that "I will not tell you that Caesar left you wonderful things in his will."

Let but the commons hear this testament—
Which, pardon me, I do not mean to read—

And they would go and kiss dead Caesar's
  wounds. (3.2.130–32)

It is not meet you know how Caesar loved
  you.
You are not wood, you are not stones, but
  men,
And, being men, hearing the will of Caesar,
It will inflame you, it will make you mad.
'Tis good you know not that you are his
  heirs,
For if you should, what would come of it?
  (141–46)

I have o-ershot myself to tell you of it.
I fear I wrong the honorable men
Whose daggers have stabbed Caesar, I do
  fear it. (150–52)

You will compel me then to read the will?
  . . .
Will you give me leave? (157, 160)

He coaxes, shies off, feigns reluctance, teases, making the crowd race ahead of him, drawing him *after them*.

The psychodynamics of this scene resemble that of act III, scene 7 of *Richard III*, where Buckingham and Richard, by refusals and posed resistances, prod the audience to demand that Richard be crowned. But that is more a play within the play, carefully staged before listeners indifferent at the outset. For a true parallel with the funeral scene, where a crowd is angry and needing assuagement, one must go to *Coriolanus*, act I, scene 1, where the Roman populace is streaming toward the Capitol to riot for bread. Menenius, the crafty aristocrat, interrupts them, jokes with them, tells them a parable. He introduces his story with self-deprecation, saying he will stale an old tale too often told. He tells it anyway, with humor, saying the stomach receives all the body's food, but distributes its effects through the body's veins and arteries. It is a Roman statement of trickle-down theory—wealth must go first to the rich, who will create work with it for the poor. But Menenius is a better propagandist than most trickle-down theorists. He takes a reviled thing, the belly, personifies it, turns it into a comic character, even makes it speak—makes it belch.

Then in stalks Caius Marctius (who later in the play becomes Coriolanus). Haughty and contemptuous, he undermines Menenius' deft manipulation of the citizens. Marctius says they are dishonorable whiners who neglect the reality of war and deserve no food. Meninus tries to calm him down.

> Nay, these are almost thoroughly
>   persuaded,
> For though abundantly they lack
>   discretion,
> Yet are they passing cowardly.
>   (1.1.199–201)

Two strategies for dealing with a mob are put on display. Marctius, wrapped up in his own valor and sense of worth, defies others to challenge his credentials. He is the fist, shaken at the crowd to silence it. He is noble, but his virtue is so dysfunctional as to have the effect of vice. Menenius opens the fist into an outstretched hand. Like Antony, he observes the people's shifting moods, plays on them, piques their interest. His speech is an interchange. He contrives to have his hearers beg him to go on. First Citizen asks, "Well, sir, what answer made the belly?" (1.1.104). Menenius stalls, and First Citizen *demands* the next part of the story: "Your belly's answer—*what*?" (112). The crowd is now asking, out of mere curiosity, that it be given the point Menenius intended to give it all along. There is a learning process at work, with Menenius as the Socratic midwife of the desired understanding.

The way the crowd responds to Coriolanus and Brutus on the one hand, to Menenius and Antony on the other, makes us, as the onstage audience's audience, appreciate the difference between leadership that issues orders and leadership that recruits cooperation. Brutus' assertions stun an initially resisting crowd into a respectful pause.

But Antony deflects the popular energy into new channels, of wholehearted action in the direction he wants to send them.

Antony is an even more artful speaker than Menenius. Both men begin with intellectual tools to engage the minds of their hearers. Menenius uses humor and narrative to create curiosity, which is an intellectual craving—it asks, "What next?" The crowd must stop and listen to find out where the story is going. Menenius uses curiosity as a kind of anaesthesia to passion—you cannot strangle a man when you are desirous of hearing what he has to say next. Menenius plays Scheherazade to the crowd's Sultan.

In the same way, Antony uses the dry and slow tools of irony, interrogation, and preterition to make the crowd question its own certitudes—about Brutus' honor, about Caesar's ambition. He makes the crowd wonder about Caesar's will—what could possibly be in it? Why won't he tell them? Antony, too, anaesthesizes the passions, creating a pause, a doubt, an aporia, before arousing new passions. The aporia may be enough for

Socrates, who wants to begin a process of knowing. But Antony wants to make his hearers *do* something. To accomplish this, say the classical rhetoricians, the orator must move from logos to ethos. Ethos establishes the character of the speaker as trustworthy. Aristotle says:

> One must look not only to the argument (*logos*), to its force and believability, but to the speaker, his nature, how he predisposes response. It affects the response, especially in political but also in judicial forums, that the speaker seem of a certain sort, and that the hearers understand how he feels about them, and—more to the point—how they feel about him. For his character is more influential in political responses.[9]

Brutus' speech was all an argument from ethos— trust my honorable character. Antony establishes his character as a plain lover of Caesar. He reaches his own aporia, known as aposiopesis, when he says he is so moved he cannot speak.

Bear with me.
My heart is in the coffin there with Caesar
And I must pause till it come back to me.
 (3.2.111–13)

Quintilian called this figure *interruptio:* "Speech interrupted by silence and hesitations."[10] He said it convinces more than shouting could. We can tell that Antony has clinched the argument from ethos when the citizens mutter to each other:

> 2 PLEBEIAN: Poor soul, his eyes are red
> as fire with weeping.
> 3 PLEBEIAN: There's not a nobler man
> in Rome than Antony.
> 4 PLEBEIAN: Now mark him, he begins
> again to speak. (3.2.121–23)

Antony does not call himself noble, as Brutus called himself honorable. Antony gets others to do it for him, and their testimony is weightier than self-praise.

Now is the time for Antony to move from ethos

to pathos—to the audience's own emotion. Aristotle wrote: "These passions are what make people, under new pressure, change their attitudes, with painful or enjoyable consequences—such passions as anger, pity, fear, and the like, or their opposites."[11] Antony will arouse pity for Caesar, anger at his killers, and fear for their own loss if they reject Caesar's bequests.

The motion toward pathos is articulated even in Antony's physical movement, by a piece of rhetorical dramaturgy. Antony on the podium—the upper level of Shakespeare's stage—is diffident at first, then ironic, then interrogatory, then teasing. Now he moves down onto the level of the listeners.

Shall I descend? And will you give me
leave? (3.2.160)

Antony has to signal what his moves mean since there would be a pause in the action while he goes, unseen, down the back stairs from the upper level.

The motion downward, from head to heart,

from mind to will, from scrutiny to action, is signaled by the programmatic opening line of his
speech on the lower level:

If you have tears, prepare to shed them
    now. (169)

There could be no more direct statement of pa-
thetic intent. If the speech above was probing,
feeling out the hearers' response, testing his way
step by step, the approach below is complicitous,
a matter of joint reminiscence and nostalgia.

You all do know this mantle. I remember
The first time ever Caesar put it on.
'Twas on a summer's evening in his tent
The day he overcame the Nervii.
    (3.2.170–73)

Caesar's cloak, once a sign of victory, will now be
the sign of his murder, bloodied as it was when
last seen over Caesar's dead body at the base of
Pompey's statue.

Antony takes the mantle up, fondles it in memory, and then reenacts with its help the assassination—at the very spot on the stage where Caesar fell. He goes from stab to stab, ticking off the killers' blows. Though Antony did not himself see them, he is given a kind of clairvoyance of their sequence.

> Look, in this place ran Cassius' dagger
>   through.
> See what a rent the envious Casca made.
> Through this, the well-beloved Brutus
>   stabbed . . .
> This was the most unkindest cut of all.
>   (3.2.174–76, 183)

"Kind" here is a closer form of kin, since Brutus was known to be Caesar's natural son. When Claudius calls Hamlet "cousin," the prince responds, "A little more than kin [as both nephew and stepson rather than cousin] and less than kind [as recognizing no family duty]" (*Hamlet* 1.2.65). Hamlet later refers to Claudius as "remorseless, treacherous, lecherous *kind*less villain," since he defied family ties by killing his brother (2.2.581).[12]

After pointing out where Brutus stabbed, Antony uses the speech's one major *image*, a personification of the blood that has been so potent in this play:

> And, as he plucked his cursed steel away,
> Mark how the blood of Caesar followed it
> As rushing out of doors, to be resolved
> If Brutus so unkindly knocked or no.
>   (177–80)

Once again, "unkindly." By now the crowd is weeping, is putty in Antony's hands. He has saved one last coup de théâtre for this moment. Plutarch said that he showed the mantle only—not the body. But Antony unveils the corpse—a bloody dummy carried on by Antony, wrapped in the mantle he now snatches off.[13] Here Antony strips away his mask of irony. The "honorable men" get their proper title—traitors.

O now you weep, and I perceive you feel
The dint of pity. These are gracious drops,
Kind souls. What? Weep you when you but
    behold
Our Caesar's *vesture* wounded? Look you
    here!
Here is *himself*—marred as you see with
    traitors. (193–97)

When Casca stabbed Caesar's body, he gave up
speech for action, saying, "Speak hands for me!"
Now the body speaks back, as Antony surrenders
his orator's office to the corpse's own eloquence:

I tell you that which you yourselves do
    know,
Show you great Caesar's wounds, poor poor
    dumb mouths,
And bid them speak for me. (223–25)

Antony has reenacted the killing of Caesar, to
arouse detestation over it. He does what the killers

had predicted would be done to *celebrate* their deed.
Cassius says after the murder:

> Stoop then and wash. How many ages hence
> Shall this our lofty scene be acted over
> In states unborn and accents yet unknown!

Brutus picks up the boast:

> How many times shall Caesar bleed in
>   sport
> That now on Pompey's basis lies along,
> No worthier than the dust!

And Cassius closes the ring:

> So oft as that shall be.
> So often shall the knot of us be called
> The men that gave their country liberty.
>   (3.1.111–18)

Antony did not wait for accents unknown to make
"Caesar bleed in sport." He made him bleed in

Roman accents before the supposedly liberated Romans, who conceive a hatred that will hunt down all Caesar's killers. Cassius' or Brutus' predictions prove true only in an unintended way. But the prophecy pronounced over Caesar's corpse by Antony, at the scene of the murder, is fulfilled to the letter:

> Over thy wounds now do I prophesy . . .
> A curse shall light upon the limbs of men,
> Domestic fury and fierce civil strife
> Shall cumber all the parts of Italy;
> Blood and destruction shall be so in use,
> And dreadful objects so familiar,
> That mothers shall but smile when they
>   behold
> Their infants quartered with the hands of
>   war,
> All pity choked with custom of fell deeds.
> And Caesar's spirit, ranging for revenge
> With Ate by his side come hot from hell,
> Shall, in these confines, with a monarch's
>   voice,

Cry havoc and let slip the dogs of war,
That this foul deed shall smell above the
   earth
With carrion men groaning for burial.
  (3.1.259, 262–75)

The spirit of Caesar, which Brutus was confident he could kill, is in fact unkillable.

Antony convinces the crowd at the funeral that he is "a plain blunt man" (3.2.217). But Shakespeare will not let us share that misconception. Antony, the man of many tricks, has dark tricks in his bag, as we learn from the proscription scene, where he quickly accedes to the demand that his nephew be killed: "Look, with a spot I damn him" (4.1.6). In this play of paired scenes and persons, the meeting of the Caesarian plotters is best gauged by its contrast with the meeting of the anti-Caesarean plotters. Those who gathered in Brutus' garden were idealistic fools, blind to their own motives. They are so feckless that Brutus does not even know what day of the month it is, or time of the day (2.1.3, 40), and the rest do not know the direction of sunrise (2.1.101–12). The conspirators change their minds—about including Cicero in their plot, about swearing an oath, about killing Antony—at the slightest word from Brutus. Cassius and Brutus whisper together and do not take the rest into their confidence (2.1.99). The others believe Brutus when he says Cicero thinks only of himself (2.1.150–52). They accept his claim that they are killing Caesar for his own good, as "a dish fit for the gods" (2.1.173).

There could not be a more complete contrast with the cold efficiency of the triumvirs as they lay out their plans. Brutus and Cassius withdraw from the company to whisper their own plans. Antony haughtily dismisses Lepidus so he can talk with Octavius behind the third man's back. They have just drawn up a list of those to be eliminated, and they are already planning to eliminate one of their own number. They are also scheming to use Caesar's name to defraud the people. Lepidus has been sent to another part of Antony's house to get Caesar's will. Antony had used the promise of that will to win over the people. Now he means to tamper with the will, "to cut off some charge in legacies" (4.1.9), diverting the assets to his own purpose.[14]

Editors like Nicholas Rowe were probably right to set this scene in Antony's house. The historical Antony had persuaded Calphurnia to turn over to him not only Caesar's will but all his private papers, including memoranda on things Caesar intended to do, which he kept in his home. Antony used these new provisions to dole out favors and solicit bribes from those being favored. Cicero and others were convinced that Antony was forging documents in this trove of papers only he could see. His home became "a factory of faked documents" and "a trading post for property exchanges."[15] Shakespeare refers to this use of a secret horde of papers when he has Antony tell Octavius:

> And let us presently go sit in counsel
> How covert matters may be best disclosed.
> (4.1.45–46)

Even the space where he was storing the papers was an affront to Antony's critics, since he had bought Pompey's house after Caesar confiscated it, and made it a resplendent scene for his criminal activities.[16]

The assassins of Caesar could not figure out how to use Cicero as an asset in their undertaking. Antony is clear-eyed and cold-blooded in his use of others. As he had manipulated the crowd at the funeral, he means to use Lepidus as a cover for his actions, but only to the point where he proves no longer useful. Then he will be treated like an animal living beyond the trouble of keeping him. Almost more chilling than the triumvirs' ticking off of people to die is Antony's description of his instrumental use of a human person:

> And though we lay these honors on this man
> To ease ourselves of divers slanderous loads,
> He shall but bear them as the ass bears
> gold,
> To groan and sweat under the business,
> Either led or driven as we point the way;
> And having brought our treasure where we
> will,

Then take we down his load, and turn him
off
Like to the empty ass to shake his ears
And graze in commons.
OCTAVIUS: You may do your will,
But he's a tried and valiant soldier.
ANTONY: So is my horse, Octavius,
and for that
I do appoint him store of provender.
It is a creature that I teach to fight,
To wind, to stop, to run directly on,
His corporal motion governed by my spirit—
And in some taste is Lepidus but so,
He must be taught and trained and bid go
forth,
A barren-spirited fellow, one that feeds
On objects, arts, and imitations
Which, out of use and staled by other men,
Begin his fashion. Do not talk of him
But as a property. (4.1.19–40)

Shakespeare shows that the great Republican
Rome had its darker side. The accomplishment of

this play is hard to exaggerate. It is the first play to bring a strong feel for Romanitas to the English stage. There had been many school exercises, in Latin and in English, many imitations of Seneca's blood-tragedies, but even Shakespeare's first Roman play, *Titus Andronicus*, was in the vein of *Gorboduc* more than of Livy. Ben Jonson knew far more about Rome than Shakespeare did (as his gibe about Shakespeare's "small Latine" shows). But his Roman plays are congested and clogged with their own learning. Shakespeare has a feel for Roman rhetoric, Stoicism, nobility, and cynicism that are immediately convincing.

Shakespeare's own company put on Jonson's two Roman plays, with Shakespeare listed as acting in *Sejanus* and probably acting in *Catiline*. But Jonson had to admit that he had a collaborator on the first one. When, later, he published his own unaided effort, it was the long play with labored references and footnotes that we read today. Anne Barton makes the convincing conjecture that Shakespeare, as the troupe's resident playwright and the author of its own successful Roman drama of 1599, was commissioned to put Jonson's 1603 tragedy in playable form.[17] Apparently even Shakespeare could not make a hit out of such recalcitrant material, but it would be interesting to see what that collaboration looked like. It is hard to imagine that it was not leaner and more focused than Jonson's own published version of 1605. The distance between Shakespeare's technique and Jonson's can be seen in the showpiece orations from *Julius Caesar* and *Catiline*. Shakespeare gives Antony the long funeral oration—170 lines—but fills the delivery with drama, pathos, crowd reactions—moving forward the action of the play, turning around the whole understanding of Brutus' oration. Jonson takes 287 lines to translate Cicero's first speech against Catiline (if Burbage had to deliver it as published, it must have tested even his great memory)—and the reaction of the audience is limited to Cato's approval, Caesar's worries, and Catiline's fears. The situation is more spelled out than changed.

Shakespeare's Rome is more convincing than Jonson's, and it suggests another contrast of an intuitive as opposed to a scholarly approach to the classics. Simon Goldhill points out that Lord Byron, the Cambridge-educated man who could read Greek, was scornful of Keats, who was ignorant of the Greek language. But Keats intuited the Greek spirit, from the Elgin marbles and from Chapman's Homer, in ways that all Byron's classical reading and travels could not equal. Even Matthew Arnold, in most ways no fan of Keats, considered the Ode on a Grecian Urn "as Greek as a thing from Homer or Theocritus."[18] What Byron was to Keats, Jonson was to Shakespeare— one man saying the other cannot do what in fact he has done. But Shakespeare's achievement is greater than Keats's. The latter saw the ideality and adventurousness of the Greek spirit, but Shakespeare saw all around the Roman ethos, its bellicose and cold-blooded side, as well as its aspirations after honor and nobility. He gives us the Roman mobs as well as the Roman snobs. He has called up, for all time, a world whose time was over.

Cassius

Parallel Lives

"Look upon this picture . . . "

Cassius says he will offer Brutus a mirror, to show him how truly noble he is. Cassius' question, "Tell me, good Brutus, can you see your face?" (1.2.51), is echoed in one of the letters tossed through Brutus' window: "Brutus, thou sleep'st; awake and *see thyself*" (2.1.46). Though the letters sent to Brutus come from "the people" in Plutarch, we know that Cassius has forged them in the play. He wants to turn Brutus' thoughts back upon himself —which shows a shrewd estimate of Brutus' self-absorption. But what Cassius sets up, instead of a mirror, is a double portrait, of Brutus paired off against Caesar:

> Brutus and Caesar: what should be in that
>   "Caesar"?
> Why should that name be sounded more
>   than yours?
> Write them together: yours is as fair a
>   name.
> Sound them: it doth become the mouth as
>   well.
> Weigh them: it is as heavy. Conjure with
>   'em:
> "Brutus" will start a spirit as soon as "Cae-
>   sar." (1.2.143–48)

It is an exercise like the one Hamlet proposes to his mother:

> Look here upon this picture, and on this—
> The counterfeit presentment of two
>   brothers.

See what a grace was seated on this brow

. . .

This was your husband. Look you, now,
   what follows.
Here is your husband, like a mildewed ear
Blasting his wholesome brother. (3.4.52–54,
   62–64)

These two plays, written in the same year, offer
us "parallel lives," at the very time when Shakespeare was immersed in the parallel lives of Greek
and Roman heroes written by Plutarch. The *Julius Caesar* comparison is meant to show that Brutus is not inferior to Caesar. The *Hamlet* passage
asserts that Claudius is far inferior to Hamlet the
elder. The technique of balancing strengths and
weaknesses is woven through all of Plutarch's bi-
ographies, which usually begin with a prologue
pointing out similarities between the Greek and
the Roman figures he is comparing, and then end
with a comparison (Greek *syngkrisis*, "joint judgment") stressing differences between them.[1] This
cross-cultural exercise is something Shakespeare

was living with all the time he mined Plutarch's lives for his Roman plays.

Plutarch's method, he tells us himself, is the same as Hamlet's method—comparing two lives *as if comparing two pictures:*

> In fact there is no better way to learn how women's strong points resemble or differ from men's than to place one life by another, one action by another, as if they were works of fine art . . . to see what is shared and what is distinct. They have different strong points, different colorations as it were, as they sort themselves out in terms of formative circumstances, physical makeup, nurture, and way of living. Achilles, for instance, has one kind of courage, Ajax another. Odysseus is not shrewd in the same way that Nestor is. Cato is not virtuous exactly as Agesilaus is.[2]

Once Cassius uses Caesar to spur on Brutus, the poising of man against man begins for all the major figures in this play. It is a drama famous for the difficulty of deciding which role to emphasize. The characters rotate around each other like the plates of a Calder mobile. Touch one and it affects the position of all others. Raise one, another sinks. But they keep coming back into a precarious balance. What is said of one will be said or thought of a counterpart. Adjusting balances back and forth is what Plutarch constantly does. He was working from a rhetorical tradition that composed *dissoi logoi* (paired pleadings). In the generation before Plutarch's the Roman historian Velleius Paterculus made these refined distinctions:

> Cassius was as much the better general as
> Brutus was the better man. Between them,
> you would want to keep Brutus for friend
> and avoid Cassius as enemy. The latter had
> more strength, the former more goodness.
> Had they prevailed, Brutus would have
> made a better ruler than Cassius, as Caesar
> was better than Antony.[3]

The characters in this play describe others in terms that are unconscious self-descriptions:

Caesar says of Cassius: "Such men as he be never at heart's ease / Whiles they behold a greater than themselves" (1.2.207–8).

Cassius confesses to what Caesar will say of him: "I had as lief not be as live to be / In awe of such a thing as I myself" (1.2.95–96).

Brutus says of Cicero: "For he will never follow anything / That other men begin" (2.1.50–51).

Plutarch says of Brutus: "Brutus might indeed have come to have been the chiefest man of Rome, if he could have contented himself for a time to have been next unto Caesar."[4]

Antony and Octavius compete for the legacy of Caesar because each of *them* wants not to be subordinate to the other. These men know that they each desire to be the foremost man in the world, which is what drives the action remorselessly forward. Caesar, after all, had to be brought down because he *was* the foremost man in the world. This play is distinctive because it has no villains. Although each leading character has his own self-interest in mind, his own pride (which he thinks of as honor), he also believes he is acting for Rome and for its fortunes. Rome eats at them, and they eat at Rome, bringing it down in the name of its own greatness. The conspirators eliminate Caesar only to see him staring back at them when they look in the mirror. The irony of Caesar's living on in his very murderers should have been clear when a plebeian shouts a response to Brutus' funeral oration: "Let *him* be Caesar" (3.2.51). Brutus begins to sound like Caesar. The latter said:

> I rather tell thee what is to be feared
> Than what I fear; for always I am Caesar.
> (1.2.211–12)

Brutus claims that he, too, is impervious to fear:

> There is no terror, Cassius, in your threats;
> For I am armed so strong in honesty
> That they pass by me as the idle wind
> Which I respect not. (4.3.66–69)

Caesar said:

> Of all the wonders that I yet have heard,
> It seems to me most strange that men
>   should fear,
> Seeing that death, a necessary end,
> Will come when it will come. (2.2.34–37)

And Brutus:

> Why, farewell, Portia. We must die,
>   Messala.
> With meditating that she must die once,
> I have the patience to endure it now.
>   (4.3.190–92)

The merging of Brutus' and Caesar's fate is brought home when the "monstrous apparition" that calls itself Brutus' evil spirit in Plutarch is given Caesar's form by Shakespeare (4.3.282). Shakespeare knew—surely from Plutarch, and probably from other sources as well—that Brutus was thought to be Caesar's natural son, since Caesar had a notorious long affair with Servilia, Brutus' mother. Shakespeare knows but does not dwell on the physical sonship of Brutus, since he wants to emphasize that Brutus was Caesar's *spiritual* heir.

The playwright passed over a chance to refer to the story of Brutus' sonship when he did not quote the only ancient account of Caesar's last words—which were, supposedly, "*Kai su, teknon*" ("Even you, *child*"). Suetonius and Dio Cassius report these words (while denying that he really said them).[5] Dio writes in Greek and could, one might think, be translating the Latin *Et tu, puer?* or *Et tu, fili?* But Suetonius writes in Latin, and his report makes it clear that Caesar's last words, according to the rumor they both report, were in Greek. Shakespeare, if he did not know these words directly, could well have known them indirectly. But he does not use them, with their possible indication that Brutus was Caesar's natural son. Instead, he uses the exclamation, *Et tu, Brute?* a Renaissance invention with no classical source.

Where did Shakespeare find this? It was suggested in the anonymous play *Caesar's Revenge*, from the 1590s—"What, Brutus too?" (line 1727). The earliest printing we have of the Latin saying is in the surviving epilogue of Richard Eedes's *Caesar Interfectus* (1582). It next occurs in the "bad quarto" (actually an Octavo) of Shakespeare's own *Henry VI, Part Three* (1595).[6] When the Duke of Clarence breaks into the presence of his brother, King Edward, as an apparent enemy, the king says:

Et tu, Brute? Wilt thou stab Caesar too?[7]

The next appearance of the Latin phrase is in the Folio text of *Julius Caesar*. Why is it lacking in the Folio text of *3 Henry VI*? Stanley Wells and Gary Taylor suggest that some accident caused a lacuna in this part of the Folio, making it less dramatic than the Octavo scene with the *Et tu, Brute* line.[8] This idea would be reinforced if John Cox and Eric Rasmussen are right in saying that the Octavo may be an early draft of Shakespeare's play copied out by an actor, not the memorial reconstruction of "bad quarto" theory.[9] But why is it in Latin? By theatrical convention we assume that all the people in the play we read in English were speaking in their native Latin. A too-sophisticated idea would be that, just as Suetonius showed a linguistic shift in making his Latin hero speak Greek at his death, Shakespeare signaled a comparable shift by making Caesar use a different tongue at the same moment. But who in the audience could have perceived this? The most we can say about *Et tu* is that Shakespeare did not take this opportunity for hinting that Brutus was Caesar's *teknon*.

Nonetheless, Brutus has begun to mirror and resemble his victim Caesar in the second half of the play. And so has Cassius. The conspirators-to-be first mocked the Caesar who "plucked me ope his doublet, and offered them his throat to cut" (1.2.265–66). But Cassius later says in the same spirit:

> There is my dagger
> And here my naked breast (4.3.100–101)

Caesar is the measure these men apply to each other and to themselves. Cassius, berated by Brutus, says,

> When Caesar lived, he durst not thus have
> moved me.

And Brutus replies:

> Peace, peace; you durst not so have
> tempted him. (4.3.58–59)

Brutus says that Cassius, who struck Caesar down "but for supporting robbers," has become a robber himself—though Brutus asks for a share of the loot (4.3.69–80). Cassius tells Brutus:

> Strike [me] as thou didst at Caesar, for I
> know
> When thou didst hate him worst, thou
> lovedst him better
> Than ever thou lovedst Cassius.
> (4.3.104–6)

In the mirroring action of this play, the conflict between the paired adversaries in the battle scenes shows a similar dynamic. Cassius takes the lead drawing Brutus into the murder, but then Brutus shoves him back from the leadership. In the same way, Antony is the stronger figure at the beginning of the triumvirate, telling Octavius they must use and discard Lepidus (4.1.12–40); but Octavius asserts total control over the battle at Philippi. This repeats the process by which Brutus first expresses reluctance to be drawn in by Cassius (1.2.63, 165–67), but then repeatedly overrules Cassius—in seven instances, any one of them posing a danger to their enterprise, and some of them entirely crippling it.

1. When Cassius says that the conspirators must swear to their plot, Brutus forbids it, saying that justice itself will vindicate them without any such bond (2.1.113–16).

2. Brutus excludes Cicero from the plot against Caesar, though Cassius urges his

inclusion (2.1.140–52). Cicero would have
delivered a better defense at Caesar's
funeral than Brutus' self-referential one.

3. Brutus rejects Cassius' argument that
   Antony should be killed along with
   Caesar (2.1.155–65). Later, when Brutus
   lashes back at Antony's taunts before
   battle, Cassius bitterly remarks.

   > Brutus, thank yourself.
   > This tongue had not offended so today
   > If Cassius might have ruled. (5.1.45–47)

   When Gielgud was playing Antony in
   1930, he broke into a "derisive laugh
   when Cassius reminded Brutus whose
   fault it was that Antony was still alive."[10]

4. Brutus gives Antony permission to speak
   at the funeral, though Cassius rightly
   says this is courting disaster:

   > You know not what you do. Do not
   >   consent

That Antony speak in his funeral.
Know you how much the people may
  be moved
By that which he will utter?
  (3.1.232–35)

5. Brutus determines that he shall speak
   first, then leave, telling the crowd to stay
   with Antony. It is a commonplace bit
   of advice to public speakers that they
   should try to speak last, if possible, lest
   an opponent raise things that cannot be
   answered in a response. (In Plutarch,
   Brutus cannot answer Antony because
   they speak on two different occasions,
   Brutus defending the assassination
   in the Forum, Antony alone at the
   funeral.)[11]

6. Brutus decides to go out to battle at
   Philippi, though Cassius rightly says
   this is yielding the advantage to their
   foe (4.3.199–212), a verdict Antony
   and Octavius endorse (5.1.1–12). That

Brutus has reduced Cassius to his own instrument is emphasized when Cassius says:

Be thou my witness that against my will
(As Pompey was) am I compelled to set
Upon one battle all our liberties.
   (5.1.73–75)

7. Brutus, though a less experienced soldier than Cassius, takes the foremost military role.[12] Though he has ordered Cassius to attack first (4.3.302–4), he charges too soon himself (5.3.5, 10), exposing Cassius to disaster. Then he loses control of his troops, who disperse their energies in looting (5.3.7).

In every case, Brutus wrested decision from Cassius, who began the process of ousting Caesar, and in every case his decision was the wrong one. Cassius had earlier been certain that he could manipulate Brutus. "I see / Thy honorable mettle may be wrought" (1.2.308–9). But it is Brutus' stubborn honor that refuses Cassius' direction after his first agreement with him. (We have seen that he needed little prompting to attack Caesar.) Cassius is too confident of his demagogic skills, which are far more successful with the supposedly skeptical Casca. These two "temptation" scenes—first with Brutus, then with Casca—make one of the many parallels, in this play, of showing "this picture and that." Cassius tells Brutus that Caesar, no better than Brutus, has become a colossus under whose legs Romans must creep (1.2.134–37). He describes for Casca

> A man no mightier than thyself or me
> In personal action, yet prodigious grown
> And fearful. (1.3.76–78)

He laments to Brutus:

> Rome, thou hast lost the breed of noble
> bloods! (1.2.150)

His words to Casca are:

> But woe the while, our fathers' minds are
> dead. (1.3.82)

Casca, first encountered as a scamp mocking Caesar and the mob, is terrified of the storm and proves malleable to Cassius' massaging. Brutus, supposedly responsive to patriotic pleadings, is not easily wrought after all. The contrast between Cassius' putative success with Brutus and his real predominance over Casca is one of the subtler pairings of the play.

As Cassius took the lead against Caesar, then let himself be overruled by Brutus, so Antony seizes the initiative for avenging Caesar but is then shoved aside by Octavius. At the parley with Brutus and Cassius, Octavius sets the terms of defiance, and orders: "Come, Antony, away" (5.1.62). He has already demanded that Antony yield him the right flank of the battle (5.1.18), though he is young and less tested in war than Antony. The right wing was traditionally the most dangerous flank of an ancient formation, since infantrymen were covered by the shields held in the left hand of the men to their right—all but the men who had no one to their right. Undisciplined troops would drift rightward, trying to protect themselves from attack on their right.

The way these men mirror one another shows how the political dynamics of an honor-fueled drive for power makes competitors resemble their opposites. This mirroring effect led Gielgud to write:

> It is always a great question in *Julius Caesar*
> how the three leading parts are to be
> balanced so as to make an effective con-
> trast. It would be interesting to have
> them alternated by three fine actors as
> the Booth brothers, I believe, once did in
> New York.[13]

The note of interchangeability in these charac-ters, of being the same though different, is struck several times. Antony says:

Cassius

I am no orator as Brutus is . . .
But were I Brutus
And Brutus Antony, there were an Antony
Would ruffle up your spirits. (3.2.217,
26–28)

On the other hand, when Caesar offers to enter-
tain the conspirators "like friends," Brutus, in an
aside, answers that "every like is not the same, O
Caesar" (2.2.128). And Cassius says (1.2.314–15):

If I were Brutus now, and he were Cassius,
He should not humor [cajole] me [as
Cassius just cajoled him].

The Women's Mirror-Roles

The way the men's acts echo each other is com-
plemented by the same dynamic in the two wives
brought into the play, Portia and Calphurnia. Each
enters wearing a nightgown, trying to draw her
husband back into the home or keep him there.
Each feels a threat to her spouse, and tries to save

him from it—Portia from the noxious night air, Calphurnia from an ill-omened visit to the Capitol. Each uses an unnatural act as her warrant—Portia the self-inflicted wound in her thigh, Calphurnia the preternatural omens of the stormy night. Both are rebuffed in their effort, excluded from the men's world that is this drama—David Daniell notes that Brutus, after using the intimate "you" throughout his exchanges with Portia in the orchard, dismisses her with the formal "thy" and "thee" (2.1.304, 306). The frightened wife with a foolhardy husband is a recurrent situation in Shakespeare—witness the wives of Hotspur and Coriolanus.

Portia and Calphurnia appear only briefly, before Caesar's death, in the early part of the play. Calphurnia has one scene, with twenty-seven lines. Portia has two scenes, with ninety-four lines. The economy of Shakespeare's casting practice suggests that the same boy played both small parts.[14] Boy actors were a rare commodity in the public theater—as opposed to performances at court or in private homes, where choristers were available.

Not any boy off the street could be recruited for the public stage. The boys needed good diction, strong memories, carrying voices, and (usually) the ability to sing and dance—the Swiss traveler who saw *Julius Caesar* in 1599 says that two boys danced and sang in the jig that followed the play. Where to get such boys? Few good families would entrust their sons to the disreputable company of actors. The Puritans were ready to pounce on the corruption of youths. The acting troupes had to give apprenticeships to the boys, with support and protection and housing. They were adopted by specific actors for the time of their apprenticeship—a time that could last only till their voices changed.

That there were *only* two boys available for *Julius Caesar* is indicated by the fact that two appear together only once (Portia and the boy Lucius at 2.4) while Calphurnia appears alone. Lucius' small part, and the smiling way Brutus treats his weakness, indicate that Lucius was probably a beginner, as boys playing boys often are in Shakespeare. But even a beginner had to have certain aptitudes to get onto the stage at all—Lucius can play an instrument (4.3.257) and he is one of the two boys dancing the final jig.

The scarcity of boys can be seen from a mere glance at the dramatis personae of the public plays. Female characters are traditionally put at the bottom of the list. They are drastically fewer than the men's parts printed above them—and even this ratio is deceiving, since doubling boys' parts was necessary, given their rarity. Whether Shakespeare gave special meaning to the presence of one actor in two roles is a matter of dispute. But having one boy play two anxious wives in very similar situations is bound, in *Julius Caesar*, to make us reflect on what binds them and what separates. Calphurnia is all fear. She lacks the resolution that Portia shows in wounding herself, and the pride Portia takes in her family, that of Cato. On the other hand, when Portia appears by day, she is so nervous that she tries to get news from the plotters before they have time to act, and she is so flustered that, not remembering what she has said to Lucius, she blurts out information she has to cover up with an irrelevant request. She is becoming more like Calphurnia moment by moment, revealing the panic that will make her die before she knows her husband's fate.

A similar-though-different use of two boys—or a boy-and-a-half, a veteran and a beginner—can be observed in the public version of *Macbeth*.[15] There, too, only one scene has both boys in it together (4.2), when Macduff's wife and her son are seen before their murder. These are two small roles, given forty-five lines and twenty-one lines, respectively. It would be wasteful to use a skilled boy to play only the small part of Lady Macduff. She is doubled by Lady Macbeth, who disappears during the long stretch from the banquet scene (3.4) to her final appearance in the sleepwalking scene (5.1).[16] There is pathos in poising the two women against each other. Lady Macbeth had said:

> I have given suck, and know
> How tender 'tis to love the babe that milks
>   me. (1.7.54–55)

But she has made herself unnatural, "unsexed," a tower of distorted strength, in the earlier parts of the play. There is a special poignancy to seeing her disintegrate in the sleepwalking scene, and that comes after we have seen the effect of her ambition on a real mother and real child in the Macduffs. The womanliness that was crushed and repressed in Lady Macbeth comes out in her final scene—after the same boy actor has played Lady Macduff's maternal scene of innocent joshing with her boy and the brutal murder of that boy.

In *Julius Caesar*, Shakespeare uses his boys' brief parts with great efficiency. Portia has described her Catonian heritage with emphasis in the orchard scene. That adds to the impact of her reported death later on. That she would outrage her body by swallowing fire is more believable after she has stabbed her own body in the thigh. Shakespeare accepts the tale Plutarch reports but rejects, that she committed suicide by holding a hot coal in her mouth till it suffocated her—a physical impossibility.[17] (Two movie Portias, Greer Garson in 1957 and Diana Rigg in 1970, omitted the wound in the thigh. Their directors apparently wanted to keep the dignity of this Stoic woman, Cato's daughter. But her babbling with Lucius shows that she is half unhinged to begin with, preparing for her grotesque suicide.)

The historical Portia died of illness (possibly of the plague) a year before the battle of Philippi.[18] But Valerius Maximus wrote that she killed herself at news of Brutus' death in that battle.[19] This was the version of the story celebrated in works like Martial's Epigram 1.42:

Of Brutus' death when frantic Portia
learned,
Her friends hid weapons while for death
she yearned.
She cried, "Who keeps me from my chosen
date?
Like Cato's daughter I shall earn my fate."
Deprived of arms, she took coals from the
fire,

And, swallowing death, completed her
   desire.
Vainly to keep her from the sword they
   tried—
Some forms of steel are not to be
   denied.

Shakespeare makes the timing and nature of Portia's death important to his drama. By having it announced to Cassius and Brutus on the eve of battle (not well before it as in Plutarch or after it as in Valerius Maximus), he accomplishes several things. Cassius' sympathy for Brutus' loss of Portia binds the two men at the moment of their reconciliation. It casts a more favorable light on Cassius, a light that strengthens through the last act. And it provides a model for the two men's paired deaths, since each abandons his own philosophy (Epicurean for Cassius, Academic for Brutus) to adopt her Stoicism. This is a perfect example of the way Shakespeare creates deep drama by combining and contradicting his sources.

Amicitia

The death of the last conspirators extends and cul-
minates the mirroring aspects of this whole play.
Each man dies by the sword he used on Caesar,
who is turning "our swords / In our own proper
entrails" (5.3.95–96). The two men die kindred
deaths—they were, in history (and in Plutarch),
brothers-in-law, a fact Shakespeare recognizes
when he has Lucius announce the arrival of "your
brother Cassius" (2.1.70). The two men address
each other as "brother" and "dear brother" after
their reconciliation scene (4.3.96, 233, 237, 248,
305). I just referred to the way each man gives up
his own philosophy to accept the Roman Stoic's
view of suicide (5.1.76–78, 102–12). The change
in Brutus is headswimmingly rapid. When Cato
had committed suicide after being conquered by
Caesar, Brutus denounced this as an "irreligious
act" (*ouk hosion ergon*, Plutarch 30). But in Shakespeare's play, immediately after he proclaims the
Old Academy doctrine against suicide, he determines to *commit* suicide. First he says:

> I know not how,
>   But I do find it cowardly and vile,
>   For fear of what might fall, so to prevent
>   The time of life—arming myself with
>   patience
>   To stay the providence of some high
>   powers
>   That govern us below. (5.1.102–7)

Then, after one quick reference to his gracing a Roman triumph, he decides that he will not live after all (5.1.110–12).

As the drama moves into its final stage, the Roman emphasis shifts from male power to male friendship. Once more there is mirroring—even between Antony and (of all people) Cassius. Antony proved his cold ruthlessness in the proscription scene, where he sacrifices his nephew and prepares Octavius to treat Lepidus like a used-up horse. But his redeeming feature is a genuine friendship with Caesar, revealed in the emotional private address to his corpse. Whatever political motives he might have had in the funeral oration, his genuine feeling for Caesar was evident. That, at least, he was not faking. And now, as elsewhere in this play, a system of symmetries comes into play. Cassius, too, is redeemed by friendship. No one could be more different from Antony in other ways. As Caesar noted in contrasting them, Cassius has no music in him, no sense of play—which is why Cassius scorns Antony as "a masquer and a reveller" (5.1.61).

But in the ultimate test, Cassius is seen to be true to his best friend (who, interestingly, is not Brutus). When he is convinced that Titinius has been captured by the foe, he says:

O, coward that I am, to live so long,
To see my best friend ta'en before my face.
   (5.3.34–35)

That the two were indeed best friends Titinius proves by killing himself over Cassius' body, after first crowning him. He salutes the man before using the sword that killed Caesar:

The sun of Rome is set. Our day is gone.
(5.3.63)

Brutus has loyal friends, as Antony and Cassius did. Indeed, he says:

My heart doth joy that yet in all my life
I found no man but he was true to me.
(5.5.34–35)

Predictably, therefore, Brutus is turned down by the first three men he asks to assist him in his suicide, and the fourth does so only in a spirit of loyal help. Meanwhile, Lucilius proves his friendship for Brutus by pretending that he is Brutus, to draw foes away from the real man (5.4.7–8). For his valor Lucilius is then befriended by Antony and Octavius (5.4.26–29, 5.5.61).

Male comradeship is the one part of the Roman ethos that gives a positive note to the politics of this play. Despite their political differences, the major characters have genuine emotional ties to their male peers, greater than those to the women in their lives. Caesar's and Antony's bond is closer than Caesar's to Calphurnia. Even Brutus shows greater tenderness and intimacy with Lucius than with Portia. The only man who betrays no emotional connection with another is, not surprisingly, Octavius. Shakespeare had read on in Plutarch and knew that the cold man who would prevail in the end was the winner in his future play, *Antony and Cleopatra*. In the macho world of Roman politics, all the heroes take hands with each other, to draw themselves down, and Rome with them. Brutus says of Cassius:

> The last of all the Romans, fare thee well.
> It is impossible that ever Rome
> Shall breed thy fellow. (5.3.99–101)

Antony says of Brutus:

> This was the noblest Roman of them all.
>   (5.5.68)

Octavius says:

> According to his virtue let us use him.
> (5.5.76)

They perish in the illusory name of Roman nobleness.

Shakespeare is nowhere truer to Rome than in the importance he places on Roman friendship. *Amicitia* was an important social-political force, more hedged about with forms and procedures than is friendship in our time. Since formal political parties did not exist then, friendship was an important social glue holding together groups in ways that transcended the rather hermetic ties of family. Friendship softened the rigors of the patronage system; it bridged the gap between classes; it supplied an egalitarian note in an otherwise hierarchical system.[20] Friends had to treat each other as equals, despite all the differences imposed on them by law and custom. It had its own mirroring effect, as Cicero noted: "Looking at a friend, one looks on a kind of representation (*exemplar*) of oneself."[21] The obligations of friendship were taken seriously. Any breach in friendship was to be regretted—Cicero called it a "heavy violation" (*gravissimum crimen*).[22] "There is something dreadful in the breaking up of friends. If a falling out should occur, the tie should rather fade away than be stamped out."[23]

Cicero's treatise on friendship (*De Amicitia*) was commonly read in the schools in Shakespeare's time.[24] It was written in the stressful last year before Cicero's murder by Antony's agents. In the aftermath of Caesar's assassination, Cicero found many of his friendships strained to the breaking point, since he had allies among the Caesarians and among the "liberators." He worked hard to keep relations firm with one of Caesar's supporters whom he had known from boyhood, Gaius Matius.[25] One of his friends in the past had been Mark Antony himself. Because of that, Cicero honored their friendship in his first speech against Antony.[26] Since friends did favors (*beneficia*) and expected favors in return, Antony, who had performed such services for Cicero, complained that Cicero was violating the terms of friendship. There was something almost sacred in the *beneficia* received and reciprocated by friends. The Roman poet Martial held no obligation greater than a friendship based on such favors:

> Since gifts to friends your friendships save,
> You keep thus always what you gave.[27]

The first thing Shakespeare's Antony says in defense of Caesar at his funeral is this:

> He was my friend, faithful and just to me.
> (3.2.85)

Loyalty (*fides*) was the supreme value in friendship. Antony repays that reliability when he says his only claim at the funeral is to be "a plain blunt man / That love my friend" (3.2.218–19). After Antony had accused Cicero of violating their friendship, Cicero had to make an elaborate defense in his *Second Philippic*. He says there that some limits have to be placed on friendship, and Antony had been the first to go beyond those limits.[28]

This was the occasion for Cicero's writing *De Amicitia*. There he describes the duties of a friend (to reassure men like Matius that they could still be close), and yet says that men cannot accept any and all conduct from their friends (defending himself against Antony and others). Friendship presumes a certain steadfast conduct in the partner. Candid criticism should be accepted from a friend. In fact, insincere approval of bad conduct destroys the basis of friendship:

> False pretense is fatal to all relations (since it renounces and clouds truthfulness), but it works most against friendship, by destroying sincerity, without which the claim of friendship means nothing. The real point of friendship is to fuse several people into a single frame of mind, and how can it do this when one of the partners is not even single in himself, but variable, dodging, and divided?[29]

The obligation to a friend lapses whenever a friend asks you to do something disgraceful, dishonorable, or wrong. It *must* be ended when the friend encourages one to act against one's country (the gravamen of Cicero's charges against Antony).[30]

In the tent scene of *Julius Caesar,* Brutus and Cassius explore many aspects of this subject. Brutus says that Cassius denied him a *beneficium.* Cassius says that Brutus is insulting, not loving, in his criticism, making much of little faults. Brutus says he cannot flatter where he sees wrong. Their exchanges exemplify much of what Cicero says in his book:

> Since it is a trait of friends to give advice
> and get advice—and since giving it should
> be done with candor and no carping, while
> getting it should be done with receptivity
> and no reproaching—there is nothing more
> harmful to friendship than feigned praise,
> ingratiation, or flattery. For whatever you
> call them, these must be counted the curse

of shifty and deceptive people, who want to be pleasant rather than truthful.[31]

Cassius is like the historical Antony, saying that Brutus' criticisms violate the code of candid (but not carping) admonition:

> Most noble brother, you have done me
>   wrong. (4.2.36)

> In such a time as this it is not meet
> That every nice offence should bear his
>   comment. (4.3.7–8)

>   Braved by his brother,
> Checked like a bondman, all his faults
>   observed,
> Set in a notebook, learned and conned by
>   rote
> To cast into my teeth. (4.3.96–99)

Brutus answers, as the historical Cicero did to Antony, that Cassius has done dishonorable things and is asking for Brutus' complicity in them:

Shall we now
Contaminate our fingers with base bribes,
And sell the mighty space of our large
honors? (4.3.23–25)

CASSIUS: A friendly eye could never see
such faults.
BRUTUS: A flatterer's would not, though
they do appear
As huge as high Olympus. (4.3.90–92)

CASSIUS: A friend should bear his
friend's infirmities,
But Brutus makes mine greater than they
are.
BRUTUS: I do not, till you practise them
on me. (4.3.86–88)

The difference between Antony-Cicero and Cassius-Brutus is that the first pair did not end in reconciliation but in Cicero's murder by Antony. Why does Brutus not keep insisting on principle as the argument winds down? Brutus tells Cassius,

> Be angry when you will, it shall have
>   scope.
> Do what you will, dishonor shall be
>   humored. (4.3.102–3)

Cicero, too, had at first said, "I will humor a friend's bent."[32] But when Antony persisted in his objectionable conduct, Cicero attacked him savagely and wrote *De Amicitia* to defend his rejection of a former friend. What makes Brutus act in a different way is the fact that he has decided to *share* in Cassius' dishonor. He says he is too honorable to take bribes himself, but he wants a cut of Cassius' "take."

> I did send to you
> For certain sums of gold, which you denied
>   me,
> For I can raise no money by vile means.
>   (4.3.69–71)

Shakespeare looks below and behind the poses of honor with which this play is filled. The vices of Rome poison even the traces of nobility left in friendship.

I commented in the previous chapter on Shakespeare's ability to intuit Rome. Nothing shows that better than his appreciation of the importance of friendship in the Roman ethical system. Perhaps he had some schoolboy memory of Cicero's *De Amicitia,* or he may have picked up echoes of it in other authors—he clearly had a capacious and tenacious memory. But his ability to grasp the ethos of a culture like that of Rome goes far beyond mere homework of Ben Jonson's sort. The book he read most surely is the human heart.

There are, I repeat, no villains in this play. Though each character has his own self-interest, and a readiness to use or do away with other characters, all think they are doing so for the honor or glory or persistence of Rome. This play is the only one that gives us all Rome all the time. Other plays show us the betrayers of Rome—*Titus Andronicus* gives us subversion by the Goths, *Antony and Cleopatra* a key defection to Egypt, *Coriolanus* a similar defection to the Volscians. Here only

Romans bring down the Roman Republic, trying to save it. It is a play that has provided us with our strongest image of Rome, a lasting image, though it tells of Roman things that perish (as all human greatness must).

Afterword

The sole textual source of Shakespeare's *The Tragedie of Julius Caesar* is the Shakespeare First Folio
(1623). I work directly from it, in Charlton Hin-
man's facsimile (New York: Norton, 1968), but
modernize the spelling and pointing. I use the
lineation in the *Riverside Shakespeare* (2nd ed., Bos-
ton: Houghton Mifflin, 1997), since that is the
basis for citations in Marvin Spevack's invaluable
Harvard Concordance to Shakespeare (Cambridge:
Belknap Press of Harvard University Press, 1973).

For his source Shakespeare was not dealing
with Plutarch's original Greek text (from the first
century CE) nor with Jacques Amyot's French

translation of that text (1559–65), but with Thomas North's translation of the Amyot translation (1579). It is important that Shakespeare encountered Plutarch at third hand, and in a very English-Renaissance garb. The editions I used are: Jacques Amyot, *Les vies des hommes illustres, novelle edition* (Paris: P. Dupont, 1826), Thomas North, *The Lives of the Noble Grecians and Romanes*, Renaissance spelling edition (Oxford: Basil Blackwell, 1928). I modernize the spelling and punctuation of North's Renaissance text.

I profited from commentary in the following modern editions of *Julius Caesar*—Cambridge 1 (1949, edited by J. Dover Wilson), Arden 2 (1955, edited by T. S. Dorsch), Oxford (1984, edited by Arthur Humphries), Cambridge 2 (1988, edited by Marvin Spevack), Everyman (1989, edited by John F. Andrews), Arden 3 (1998, edited by David Daniell), Yale (2006, edited by Burton Raffel). Barbara Gaines, director of the Chicago Shakespeare Theater, and John Andrews, president of the Shakespeare Guild, read the whole manuscript and made valuable suggestions.

Notes

ONE
Caesar

1. Here are the line counts for the leading figures in the play: Brutus 738; Cassius 513; Antony 361; Caesar 155; Casca 139. See T. J. King, *Casting Shakespeare's Plays: London Actors and Their Roles, 1590–1642* (Cambridge: Cambridge University Press, 1992), 199.

2. Plutarch, *The Lives of the Noble Greecians and Romanes*, trans. Thomas North, 8 vols. (Oxford: Blackwell, 1928), *Cicero* 5, 24–27, 30. I cite North's Plutarch from the Shakespeare Head Press edition, but I modernize the spelling and pointing.

3. North, *Antonius* 20.

4. Martial, Epigram 5.71:

> The worst death you contrived
> Was Cicero's harsh end.
> The man of treasured words

> To silence you did send.
> This is the just reward
> For punishment so grim:
> Since you tore out his tongue,
> All tongues will speak of him.

Also, Martial, Epigram 1.60:

> Pothinus matched Mark Antony in crime:
> They slew the noblest Romans of their time.
> The helpless victims they decapitated,
> An act of infamy with shame related.
> One head was Pompey's, who brought
>   triumphs home,
> The other Cicero's, the voice of Rome.
> Pothinus acted for another man, on hire.
> Mark Antony indulged his own desire.

Translations from the Latin texts are my own unless otherwise specified.

5.   North, *Brutus* 8.

6.   North, *Cicero* 24.

7.   On *Caesar's Revenge*, see Ernest Schanzer, "A Neglected Source of *Julius Caesar*," *Notes and Queries* 1999 (1954): 196–97, and Jacqueline Pearson, "Shakespeare and 'Caesar's Revenge,'" *Shakespeare Quarterly* 32 (1981): 101–3.

8.   North, *Brutus* 37.

9.   Epic uses of the teikhoskopia are at *Iliad* 3.151–244, *Aeneid* 12.134–60, and *Paradise Lost* 3.56–134. Dramatic uses are Euripides, *The Phoenician Women* 88–201, Marston, *Antonio and Mellida* 1.1.98–1541, Jonson, *Sejanus* 1.105–95, and Shakespeare, *Troilus and Cressida* 1.3.179–250.

10. See, for instance, David Daniell, the Arden *Julius Caesar* (1998), 13–15, and James Shapiro, *A Year in the Life of William Shakespeare, 1599* (New York: HarperCollins, 2005).

11. Hamlet speaks 819 lines, and Henry V 1,056, second only to Richard III's 1,062. See King, *Casting Shakespeare's Plays*, 206, 196, 162.

12. North, *Caesar* 69, 17.

13. Ibid., 17.

14. Ibid., 49.

15. Suetonius, *The Deified Julius* 54.

16. North, *Marcus Cato* 20.

17. Suetonius, *Nero* 34.

18. *Odyssey* 12.42–25, *Aeneid* 1.118.

19. North, *Caesar* 18, 19.

20. North, *Antonius* 60. And see Christopher Pelling, "Plutarch on Caesar's Fall," in *Plutarch and His Intellectual World: Essays on Plutarch*, ed. Judith Mossman (London: Duckworth, 1997), 215–32.

21. North, *Dion-Brutus Comparison* 2. Earlier in this sequence Plutarch said that the gods denied favorable news to Brutus—of his side prevailing at sea—to prevent him from winning on land: "The state of Rome (in my opinion) being now brought to that pass that it could no more abide to be governed by many lords but required one only absolute government: God, to prevent Brutus that it should not come to his government, kept this victory from his knowledge" (North, *Brutus* 47). And see North, *Caesar* 57: "And now for [Caesar] himself, after he had ended his civil wars, he did so honorably behave himself that there was no fault to be found in him: and therefore methinks, amongst other honors they gave him, he rightly deserved this, that they should build him a temple of clemency, to thank

him for his courtesy he had used unto them in his victory. For he pardoned many of them that had borne arms against him." Even the regicidally republican John Milton agreed with Plutarch that Rome needed an autocrat, condemning "the error of the noble Brutus and Cassius, who felt themselves of spirit to free a nation, but considered not that the nation was not fit to be free." Cited in Charles Martindale and Michelle Martindale, *Shakespeare and the Uses of Antiquity* (London: Routledge, 1994), 147.

22. North, *Brutus* 6.

23. From a vast literature, excellent samples are Leeds Barroll, "Shakespeare and Roman History," *Modern Language Review* 53 (1958): 327–43, and George K. Hunter, "A Roman Thought: Renaissance Attitudes to History Exemplified in Shakespeare and Jonson," in *An English Miscellany: Presented to W. S. Mackie*, ed. Brian S. Lee (Cape Town: Oxford University Press, 1977), 92–117.

24. Ben Johnson, *Sejanus His Fall* 1.407–9.

25. North, *Caesar* 69: "Above all, the ghost that appeared unto Brutus shewed plainly, that the gods were offended with the murther of Caesar."

26. Francis Bacon, "Of Revenge," in *The Essays*, ed. John Pitcher (Harmondsworth: Penguin, 1985), 73.

27. North *Antonius* 59–60; and see Pelling, "Plutarch on Caesar's Fall."

28. Francis Bacon, *Imago Civilis Julii Caesaris*, in *The Works of Francis Bacon*, ed. James Spedding, Robert Leslie Ellis, and Douglas Denon Heath, 14 vols. (London: Longmans, 1862–1901), vol. 6, "Appian, *Civil Wars*" 2.130.

29. North, *Caesar* 57.

30. Ibid., 66.

31. Samuel Johnson, *Johnson on Shakespeare*, ed. Arthur Sherbo, 2 vols. (New Haven: Yale University Press, 1968), 2: 830.

32. René Girard has a rich treatment of the sacrifice theme in the play: *A Theater of Envy* (South Bend, Ind.: St. Augustine's, 2004), 200–220.

33. North, *Caesar* 69.

34. North, *Brutus* 36.

35. David Daniell, Introduction to *Julius Caesar*, Arden Shakespeare (Walton-on-Thames: Thomas Nelson, 1998), 115.

36. Ibid.

37. Marvin Spevack, Introduction to *Julius Caesar*, updated ed. (Cambridge: Cambridge University Press, 2003), 42.

TWO
Brutus

1. Cicero wrote to Brutus, "I am proud of your reputation as a speaker" (*De Oratore* 6.24). The books dedicated to him are *Brutus* and *Orator*.

2. Brian Vickers, *Classical Rhetoric in English Poetry*, new ed. (Carbondale: Southern Illinois University Press, 1970), 44.

3. Wolfgang G. Müller, *Ars Rhetorica* und *Ars Poetica*: Zum Verhältnis von Rhetorik und Literatur in der englischen Renaissance," in *Renaissance-Rhetorik*, ed. Heinrich F. Plett (Berlin: De Gruyter, 1993), 230: "There was a total identification of rhetoric and poetry in the theoreticians of the Renaissance."

4. Seneca the Elder wrote a book of *Suasoriae* (Persuasions, c. 40 CE), a set of exercises beloved by the poet Ovid, who had a great impact on Shakespeare.

5. John W. Velz, "*Orator* and *Imperator* in *Julius Caesar*:

Style and the Process of Roman History," *Shakespeare Studies* 15 (1982): 63.

6. Colin Burrow, *The Oxford Shakespeare: Complete Sonnets and Poems* (Oxford: Oxford University Press, 2002), 242.

7. T. W. Baldwin, *William Shakspere's Small Latine and Lesse Greeke*, 2 vols. (Urbana: University of Illinois Press, 1944), 165.

8. Quintilian defined a *figura* as any locution that goes beyond an obvious and ordinary statement (*Institutio Oratoria* 9.1.11, 14).

9. The treatises in English that I have consulted are:

> 1532   Leonard Cox, *The Art or Crafte of Rhetoryke* (London: Robert Redman)
> Richard Sherry, *A Treatise of Schemes and Tropes* (London: J. Day)
> Henry Peacham, *The Garden of Eloquence* (London: H. Jackson)
>
> 1553   Thomas Wilson, *The Arte of Rhetorique* (London: John Kinston), ed. Peter E. Medine (University Park: Pennsylvania State University Press, 1993)
>
> 1586   Angel Day, *The English Secretarie* (London: Thomas Orwin)
>
> 1588   Abraham Fraunce, *The Arcadian Rhetorike* (London: Thomas Orwin), ed. Ethel Seaton (Oxford: Basil Blackwell, 1950)
>
> 1589   George Puttenham, *The Arte of English Poesie* (London: Thomas Orwin), ed. Gladys Doidge Willcock and Alice Walker (Cambridge: Cambridge University Press, 1936)

1599   John Hoskyns, *Direccions for Speech and Style* (Harleian Manuscript 604), ed. Louise Brown Osborn in *The Life, Letters, and Writings of John Hoskyns, 1566–1638* (New Haven: Yale University Press, 1937)

More such treatises can be found in Baldwin, *William Shakspere's Small Latine and Lesse Greeke*, 2: 29–68. A brief but incisive treatment of these works is at Vickers, *Classical Rhetoric in English Poetry*, 105–16.

10. Cicero, *De Oratore* 3.200. Quintilian tried to take an Occam's razor to the thick growth of Greek terms for tropes and figures, with only moderate success—*Institutio Oratoria* 9.1.22.

11. He finds thirty-six figures in Antony's longer oration. Jean Fuzier, "Rhetoric *Versus* Rhetoric: A Study of Shakespeare's *Julius Caesar*, Act III, Scene 2," *Cahiers Elisabethains* 5 (1974): 25–65.

12. Quintilian calls this *gradatio*, and gives an example from Demosthenes' *De Corona* 179: "I did not speak without making a proposal, did not make a proposal without acting on it, did not act on it without winning Thebans to it"—*Institutio Oratoria* 9.3.54.

13. What the Greeks called *antimetabole* ("reverse interchange") or *khiasmos* ("khi-ing"), some Romans called *commutatio* ("interchange"), *regressio* ("step back," going from a-b to b-a), or *chiasmus*. Elizabethan rhetoricians used those terms, and tried to add more vernacular descriptions. Puttenham (208) called the figure a "counterchange" (making words "to change and shift one into other's place"). Wilson (228) called it "regression." Day (95) sticks with the Latin *commutatio*. Peacham (164) defines *antimetabole* as "a scheme of speech which

inverts a sentence by the contrary." This is like Hoskyns' "a sentence inversed or turned back."

14. Quintilian, *Instututio Oratoria* 9.3.85:

> Non ut *edam* VIVO
> Set ut VIVAM *edo*.

15. Thomas Playfere's sermon was "A Most excellent and Heavenly Sermon" (1595). Playfere was capable of sentences like "Perfectly unperfect when they begin, unperfectly perfect when they end" ("The Pathway to Perfection," 1611).

16. Thomas Wilson (227) had made fun of jinglers who said things like "There is a difference between an horse mill and a millhorse." Abraham Lincoln said that Stephen Douglas was trying to "prove a horse chestnut to be a chestnut horse." *Abraham Lincoln: Speeches and Writings, 1832–1858* (New York: Library of America, 1989), 511.

17. See, in the same play (1.3.223–24):

> Thy friends suspect for traitors while thou
> liv'st,
> And take deep traitors for thy dearest friends.

18. The string of chiasms is at 4.3.352–59:

> Then fools you were these women to forswear,
> Or, keeping what is sworn, you will prove fools.
> For wisdom's sake, a word that all men love,
> Or for love's sake, a word that loves all men,
> Or for men's sake, the authors of these women,
> Or women's sake, by whom we men are men,
> Let us once lose our oaths to find ourselves,
> Or else we lose ourselves to keep our oaths.

19. Brutus uses a chiasm in the tent scene, arguing with Cassius: "Remember March, the Ides of March remember" (4.3.18).

20. Lucius Annaeus Seneca, *Oratorum et Rhetorum: Sententiae, Divisiones, Colores*.

21. Hoskyns may be remembering Quintilian: "*Like a peddler of eloquence* he will set out whatever is easy of thought, slick of phrase, tickling of ornament, grand of comparison, or overwrought in the writing—to be inspected and, as it were, pawed over" (*Institutio Oratoria* 8.3.12).

22. Francis Bacon, "Of the Colours of Good and Evil," in *Essais* (London: William Jaggard, 1606). Costard in *Love's Labor's Lost* gives a perfect division (1.1.202–12) to answer how he was caught in the "manner" (handiwork) of wooing.

> In *manner*,
> and *form*,
> *following*, sir, all those three.
> I was seen with her in the *manor* house,
> sitting with her on the *form*,
> and taken *following* her into the park,
> which, put together, is "in manner and form following."
> Now, sir, for the *manner*, it is the manner of a man to speak to a woman;
> for the *form*, in some form.
> BEROWNE: For the "*following*" sir?
> COSTARD: As it shall follow in my correction.

Love's Labor's Lost, as one long joke on rhetoric, has many foolish "divisions." A standard (if mechanical) form of amplification by partition was to consider a string of questions like: "When?" "Where"? Why?" Ferdinand reads a letter in which Don Armado describes his perambulation (1.1.235–46):

> The time, *when*?
> About the sixth hour [subdividing the division],
> when beasts most graze,
> birds best peck,
> and men sit down to that nourishment which is
>   called supper. . . .
> Now for the ground, *which*? Which, I mean, I
>   walked upon.
> It is ycleped thy park.
> Then for the place, *where*? Where, I mean, I
>   did encounter that obscene
> and most preposterous event that draweth from
>   my snow-white pen the
> ebon-colored ink which here [subdividing the
>   division]
> thou viewest,
> beholdest,
> surveyest,
> or seest.
> But to the place, *where*?
> It standeth [subdividing the division]
> north-north-east
> and by east
> from the west
> corner of thy curious-knotted garden.

Don Armado outdoes even this absurd division later in the play, in another letter, read by Boyet (4.1.64–83).

The magnanimous and most illustrate King
Cophetua set eye upon the pernicious and
indubitate beggar Zenelophon, and he it was
that might rightly say, *Veni, vidi, vici*, which to
annothanize in the vulgar—O base and obscure
vulgar!—*videlicet*, he came, saw, and overcame.
He came, one; saw, two; overcame, three. Who
came? The King. Why did he come? To see.
Why did he see? To overcome. To whom came
he? To the beggar. What saw he? The beggar.
Who overcame he? The beggar. The conclusion is victory. On whose side? The King's.
The captive is enriched. On whose side? The
beggar's. The catastrophe is a nuptial. On
whose side? The King's? No, on both in one,
or one in both. I am the King, for so stands
the comparison, thou the beggar, for so wit-
nesseth thy lowliness. Shall I commend my
love? I may. Shall I enforce thy love? I could.
Shall I entreat thy love? I will. What shall thou
exchange for rags? Robes. For tittles? Titles.
For thyself? Me.

23. So Evans (1.1.136–42) in *The Merry Wives of Windsor*.
24. *Twelfth Night* 1.5.244–49, *1 Henry IV* 1.1.131–39, *As
You Like It* 2.7.139–66, *Comedy of Errors* 3.2.103–24,
Love's Labors Lost 3.1.40–45, *Much Ado About Nothing*
5.189–92. The last case is answered in what Claudio
calls "his own *division*." In other examples, Jaques gives
the range of melancholies, and Touchstone the seven
causes of a quarrel (*As You Like It* 4.1.10–15, 5.4.49–
90). The Porter lists the three effects of drink (*Macbeth*
2.3.5–35). Lysander lists the six thwarters of true love
(*Midsummer Night's Dream* 1.1.34–49), Ulysses the

blessings of political order (*Troilus* 1.3.83–136), and Portia the blessings of mercy (*Merchant of Venice* 4.1.184–202).

25. Don J. Kraemer, Jr., "'Alas, thou hast misconstrued every thing': Amplifying Words and Things in *Julius Caesar*," *Rhetorica* 9 (1991): 169.

26. Aristotle used *taxis* for the general ordering of a speech's parts (*Rhetorica* 1414a), but later rhetoricians used it more narrowly of "pairings."

27. Kraemer, "'Alas, thou hast misconstrued every thing,'" 171.

28. Quintilian, *Instututio Oratoria* 9.2.72.

29. G. K. Chesterton, *Five Types* (New York: Henry Holt, 1911), 50–51. Compare Chesterton, *Fancies Versus Fads* (New York: Dodd, Mead, 1923), 91: "Prose is not the freedom of poetry; rather, prose is the fragments of poetry. Prose, at least in the prosaic sense, is poetry interrupted, held up and cut off from its course; the chariot of Phoebus stopped by a block in the Strand."

30. Brian Vickers, *The Artistry of Shakespeare's Prose* (London: Routledge, 1968), 243.

31. Quintilian, *Instututio Oratoria* 9.3.102.

32. Vickers, *Shakespeare's Prose*, 433.

33. For putting a "cause and quarrel" to adjudication, see *King John* 5.7.91.

34. Plutarch, *The Lives of the Noble Greecians and Romanes*, trans. Thomas North, 8 vols. (Oxford: Blackwell, 1928), *Caesar* 4, 13, 28, 31, 35, 57, 60. North is translating Amyot, who uses terms like *couleur* or *couverture* (*Vie de Jules Cesar*). Amyot in turn was translating Plutarch's Greek words like *prophasis* (pretext) or its synonyms. "Color" for "pretext" is the sense at *Cymbeline* 3.1.50.

35. Bacon, "Of the Colours of Good and Evil," 224. Thomas

Wilson (203) equated "colors" with rhetorical "ornaments."

36. On Bacon's use of "popularity," see James Shapiro, *A
Year in the Life of William Shakespeare: 1599* (New York:
HarperCollins, 2005), 128–29. Bacon advised his friend
the Earl of Essex to "speak against popularity" and condemned Caesar's "desire of popularity." Bacon knew
that *popularis* was used of a Roman leader who culti-
vated the people. When Cicero wants to condemn a
demagogue, he calls him *homo popularis*.

37. Michael Winterbottom, Introduction to Seneca, *Dec-
lamations*, trans. Winterbottom, 2 vols. (Cambridge:
Harvard University Press, 1974), 1: xviii.

38. Quintilian, *Instututio Oratoria* 4.2.88–96.

39. Bacon, "Of the Colours of Good and Evil," 239.

40. Quintilian, *Instututio Oratoria* 8.5.27–29.

41. North, *Brutus* 13.

42. Some think the two reports of Portia's death are rem-
nants of two different texts, but David Daniell makes
a strong argument against this in the Arden edition,
137–43.

43. Johnson, rejecting Warburton's emendation "if that
the fate of men" for "if not the face of men," wrote:
"'The face of men' is the 'countenance,' the 'regard,'
the 'esteem' of the public; in other terms, 'honor ' and
'reputation'; or, 'the face of men' may mean the de-
jected look of the people." *Johnson on Shakespeare*, ed.
Arthur Sherbo, 2 vols. (New Haven: Yale University
Press, 1968), 2: 828.

44. Bate makes a good case that the earliest reported stage
business for the play, by the troupe that toured Ger-
many before 1620, kept to the original direction: "Now
Titus falls upon his knees and begins to chant a dirge,

all the others sitting down by the heads. Titus takes up his hand, holds it up and looks to heaven, sobs and repeats the oath softly; he beats his breast and at the conclusion of the oath sets the hand aside. Then he takes up one head and then the other, swearing by each one in turn. Finally he goes to his daughter, who is kneeling, and swears by her also, as he did with the others, whereupon they all rise again." Jonathan Bate, Introduction to *Titus Andronicus*, Arden Shakespeare (London: Routledge, 1995), 46.

45. North, *Caesar* 29.

THREE
Antony

1. William H. Herndon and Jesse W. Weik, *Herndon's Life of Lincoln* (Cambridge, Mass.: Da Capo, 1983), 269–70.

2. Arkhilokhos 201 (West)—a chiasm. Cf. Isaiah Berlin, *The Hedgehog and the Fox* (1953; rpt. Beaverton, Ore.: Touchstone, 1983).

3. Francis Bacon, "Of the Colours of Good and Evil," in *Essais* (London: William Jaggard, 1606).

4. Cicero, *Brutus* 185.

5. Cicero, *Orator* 113.

6. Ibid., 202.

7. Plutarch, *The Lives of the Noble Greecians and Romanes*, trans. Thomas North, 8 vols. (Oxford: Blackwell, 1928), *Antonius* 14.

8. North, *Brutus* 20.

9. Aristotle, *Rhetoric* 11377b. For the relationship between logos, ethos, and pathos, see ibid. 1355b–1356a. Ethos is well discussed by D. A. Russell, *Greek Declama-*

       tion (Cambridge: Cambridge University Press, 1983), 87–105.

10. Quintilian, *Institutio Oratoria* 9.2.71.

11. Aristotle, *Rhetoric* 1378a.

12. As Johnson put it, Hamlet is saying "that he was somewhat more than cousin, and less than son." *Johnson on Shakespeare*, ed. Arthur Sherbo, 2 vols. (New Haven: Yale University Press, 1968), 2: 961.

13. In Appian, the body itself is uncovered, but there is also a bloody dummy that is lifted up on a revolving platform, to show all the wounds (*Civil Wars* 2.147).

14. For Antony's tampering with Caesar's will, see North, *Antonius* 16.

15. Cicero, *Oratio Philippica Secunda* 36: "*falsorum chirographorum officina, . . . vectigalium flagitiossismae nundinae.*" For more on forged Caesar documents, see ibid., 97–100.

16. Ibid., 60–64.

17. Anne Barton, *Ben Jonson, Dramatist* (Cambridge: Cambridge University Press, 1984), 93–94. Barton notes that the King's Men had already shortened Jonson's comedy *Every Man Out of His Humour* in 1599, and it was likely to have been even more critical of *Sejanus*, as Jonson's first attempt at tragedy.

18. Simon Goldhill, *Who Needs Greek?* (Cambridge: Cambridge University Press, 2002), 188–90.

FOUR

Cassius

1. That the paired lives were meant to be read as a single work is seen from the fact that the second one normally has, in its first sentence, the particle *de*, the second

member of the antithetical pairing *men . . . de*. Its force at the beginning of the second biography is to say "in this other case." The fact that the life of Caesar as it has come down to us lacks this *de* is one of many indications that the opening paragraphs are lost.

2. Plutarch, *The Strong Points of Women* (243 C). Plutarch used the comparative method constantly, not only in his *Parallel Lives* but in his *Philosophical Essays (Moralia)*, comparing philosophers, comic dramatists, men and women, and so on. Plutarch's strategy is well characterized by David Sansone in *Plutarch: The Lives of Aristeides and Cato* (Warminster: Aris and Phillips, 1989), 9: "What Plutarch does in his *Parallel Lives* is to select subjects in such a manner that he can explore the ways in which similar personalities react to different circumstances, and the ways in which similar circumstances are responded to by different personalities. This procedure inevitably focuses attention upon that intersection of character and environment that is the concern of the study of ethics."

3. Velleius Paterculus, *Roman History* 1.72.

4. Plutarch, *The Lives of the Noble Greecians and Romanes*, trans. Thomas North, 8 vols. (Oxford: Blackwell, 1928), *Brutus* 8.

5. Suetonius, *Vita Divi Iulii* 82; Dio Cassius, *Roman History* 44.19.

6. Also known as *The True Tragedie of Richard, Duke of Yorke*.

7. This is at 2483–86 in the Oxford edition of the Octavo.

8. Stanley Wells and Gary Taylor, *William Shakespeare: A Textual Companion* (New York: Oxford University Press, 1987), 204: "O[ctavo] seems so theatrically superior here that we must suppose either that a lacuna occurs in F (possibly the result of eyeskip from the initial C in

the manuscript speech-prefix Clarence ... or, more probably, that O here reflects revision between the foul papers, which lie behind F, and the prompt-book, from which O, indirectly, derives."

9. John D. Cox and Eric Rasmussen, Introduction to *King Henry VI, Part 3* (London: Arden Shakespeare, 2001), 166.

10. Ronald Hayman, *John Gielgud* (New York: Random House, 1971), 58–59.

11. North, *Caesar* 67, *Antonius* 14.

12. Plutarch (*Brutus* 40) says that Brutus demanded to lead the right wing, though Shakespeare has Octavius make that demand to Antony.

13. John Gielgud, *Acting Shakespeare* (New York: Scribner, 1991), 80. The three Booth brothers did act together once, in a benefit performance of *Julius Caesar*—Edwin as Brutus, John Wilkes as Antony, and Junius Brutus as Cassius. But they played it only that one time, so there could have been no opportunity of rotating the roles. Gielgud may have had a confused memory of the way Edwin Booth and Henry Irving alternated the roles of Othello and Iago in 1881. (Gielgud knew a great deal of theatrical lore because of his Terry family connections.) Gielgud refers to the *three* leading roles in *Julius Caesar*, apparently thinking that Caesar has too few lines for a leading actor to include the role in a rotation scheme, despite his own success as Caesar in 1977. At various times Gielgud successfully played Caesar, Antony, and Cassius—but never, surprisingly, Brutus. The respected drama critic J. C. Trewin said of his Cassius in 1950, "It is the performance of the season, and—I would say—the Shakespearean performance of the year" (Hayman, *John Gielgud*, 173).

14. The boy actor has a space of thirty-two lines (and a

thunderstorm) to go from Brutus' "Leave me with haste," slip into a different nightgown, and enter as Calphurnia. Then he has a space of thirty-seven lines to come back as Portia in day clothes.

15. To suggest their unnatural character, the witches are played by men, as we see from 1.3.46–48:

> You should be women,
> And yet your beards forbid me to interpret
> That you are so.

Middleton's new parts for Hecate and three graceful witches, with song and dance, were clearly added for a private performance with choristers.

16. People remember Lady Macbeth as having a longer role than her actual lines warrant. But for the sleep-walking scene, she is absent from the whole second half of the play. "Measured in lines of dialogue, Lady Macbeth has a small part, only about 10 percent of the play's spoken lines"—A. R. Braunmuller, Appendix to *Macbeth*, New Cambridge Shakespeare (Cambridge: Cambridge University Press, 1997), 266. It was easy for her to double the small part of Macduff's wife. Macduff's son would double Fleance (eight lines), and both boy actors would appear in the procession of future kings (five lines and eight lines, respectively). Orson Welles, having a supply of women actors at Republic Studios, had Lady Macbeth and Lady Macduff appear together in his movie of the play, against the text of Shakespeare.

17. North, *Brutus* 53.

18. Portia's illness and death are reported in Cicero's correspondence (*Ad Brutum* 1.9.2, 1.17.7). See John Moles, "Plutarch, Brutus, and Brutus' Greek and Latin Let-

ters," in *Plutarch and His Intellectual World: Essays on Plutarch*, ed. Judith Mossman (London: Duckworth, 1997), 141–68.

19. Valerius Maximus, *Libri Novem* 4.6.5. And see Peter Howell, *A Commentary on Book One of the Epigrams of Martial* (London: Athlone, 1989), 199–203.

20. David Konstan, *Friendship in the Classical World* (Cambridge: Cambridge University Press, 1997), 122–48.

21. Cicero, *De Amicitia* 23.

22. Cicero, *Oratio Philippica Secunda* 3.

23. Cicero, *De Amicitia* 76.

24. In the widely imitated Eton system, *De Amicitia* was read in the fifth form. Extracts and summaries of it were also taught. T. W. Baldwin, *William Shakespeare's Small Latine and Lesse Greek*, 2 vols. (Urbana: University of Illinois Press, 1944), 2: 579–81, 591–93.

25. Cicero, *Epistulae ad Familiares* 11.27–28.

26. Cicero, *Oratio Philippica Prima* 11, 12, 26, 28.

27. Martial, *Epigrammata* 5.42.

28. Cicero, *Oratio Philippica Secunda* 3–9.

29. Cicero, *De Amicitia* 92.

30. Ibid., 40–45.

31. Ibid., 91.

32. Cicero, *Oratio Philippica Prima* 28.

Index

Index